MARK FERGUSON

Build a Commercial Real Estate Empire

How to Scale to New Heights With the Right Financing, Deals, and Strategies

First edition

This book was professionally typeset on Reedsy.
Find out more at reedsy.com

Contents

I   Commercial Real Estate Strategies

1	Intro	3
2	How I got Into Commercial Real Estate	7
3	Start Big or Small?	15
4	The Basics of Commercial Real Estate	23
5	Commercial Versus Multifamily	34
6	What Type of Commercial Properties Do I Like?	38
7	Where Should You Buy Commercial Rentals?	45

II   Commercial Numbers, Analysis, and How To

8	What Makes a Deal a Deal	51
9	What Is the CAP Rate, and Why Is It So Important?	56
10	How to Find Deals on Commercial Real Estate	64
11	Financing Commercial Real Estate	71
12	Commercial Appraisals	78
13	How to Find Tenants and Manage Properties	93
14	How does Tenant Improvement (TI) work?	104
15	Commercial Leases	110
16	Repairs and Contractors	117
17	Be Prepared for the Waiting Game!	132
18	Taxes, Opportunity Zones, and 1031 Exchanges	135
19	Working with Partners and Syndication	152

III Case Studies

20 Case Study #1: My First Commercial Property   163

21 Case Study #2: 7,000-Square-Foot Office Building   166

22 Case Study #3: A Steal From Facebook   176

23 Case Study #4: One of My Best Deals Ever   183

24 Case Study #5: $2 Million? Was I Ready?   188

25 Case Study #5 Part 2: Adding Millions in Value   198

26 Case Study #5 Part 3: BRRR on a Big Scale   210

27 Case Study #6: Vacant for How Long?   218

28 Case Study #7: My First Mixed Use   222

29 Case Study #8: History in the Making   229

30 Case Study #9: Don't Ignore the Small Deals   235

31 Case Study #10: "The Compound"   238

IV My Future Plans

32 My Plan to Buy One Million Square Feet of Rentals   245

33 New Deals and Missed Deals   253

34 Finishing Thoughts on Commercial Real Estate   257

I

Commercial Real Estate Strategies

*There are many types of commercial real estate and many ways
to invest. I will go over the strategies I like to use and why.*

1

Intro

Many people have asked me to write a book about commercial real estate. I started my rental property investing career with residential properties, and I even used to suggest that most people not invest in commercial real estate, mostly because it is a very complicated business. Then, I started investing in commercial real estate and completely contradicted myself!

To be honest, commercial real estate is complicated. It is not easy, and I am still learning about the ins and outs of commercial deals. I feel I have learned enough to write a book on commercial real estate after doing a number of deals ranging from 900 square feet and $70,000 to 68,000 square feet and several million dollars.

While I am more bullish on commercial real estate, it took me many years to learn the basics. I wish I would have known much of what I do now when I started, and I hope to provide that information in this book. I can remember sitting in meetings with my commercial real estate brokers, nodding my head in agreement to what they were saying, even though I had no clue what they were talking about. I wanted them to take me seriously, and if I admitted I did not know what "TI" was, they may not do that.

That meeting was for the 2.1-million-dollar commercial property I was buying, and I thought to myself, "Should I really be buying the most expensive property of my life when I don't really have a clue what these guys are talking about?" I trusted my gut, got the deal done, and it was the best deal I ever did.

I have done many deals where I did not have all the facts before jumping in. Some have worked out great and others not so great, but it has been a fun and an amazing learning experience. While doing is often the best way to learn, I still think I could have done much better if I had a book like this to teach me how commercial real estate works and how to get deals done.

I have read many real estate books, including many that involve commercial real estate, but most of those books are very high level. They talk about huge deals and big numbers, but they don't talk about how to build up to those deals or how to get those deals done. You have to know many things in the commercial real estate world. A few things that are vitally important are:

·Leases.
  ·CAP rates.
  ·TI or tenant improvement, which I had to look up after our meeting!
  ·Zoning.
  ·Financing.
  ·Networking.
  ·Analyzing deals.
  ·Property Management.
  ·Much more.

Okay, so that was more than a few things, but that is how commercial real estate works. As soon as you think you have it figured out, you learn something new that changes everything!

The really cool thing about commercial real estate is that it is complicated and there are so many things to know. That is the reason I love real estate in general. A computer program cannot figure out real estate—there are too many variables. The more complicated something is, the fewer the people are who enter the business. The more complicated the business, the more opportunity there is for those who master it or at least are willing to learn a little but more than the next guy!

There is a lot of opportunity in commercial real estate. The main reason I started buying commercial real estate was I could no longer find decent rentals in the residential sector. Prices were too high, and rents were too low to make decent money.

After searching in other states for new markets to invest in, I discovered commercial. I realized that not nearly as many investors were willing to buy commercial real estate and that you could make money on it! 100, instant-money-making deals weren't just sitting on the market, but opportunities popped up occasionally.

I could cash flow with commercial properties, and I could add value to them as well. In fact, there was much more opportunity to add value to commercial properties than residential.

When I talk about commercial real estate, I am not talking about multi-unit apartments. I mean real commercial—grocery stores, office buildings, dance studios, restaurants, coffee shops—places where business is done, not places where people live.

There is opportunity to make money with apartment buildings, and I know many people who make a killing at it, but this book is about straight commercial real estate. Personally, I like commercial better than residential because it can be easier to manage, there are fewer expenses, the tenants are easier to work with, and it can be easier to find deals.

In this book, I will not only teach you many of the terms you need to know, the ways to get deals, how to meet the right people, and how to add value, but I will also go over many of my commercial deals and what I did every step of the way to buy them and make money with them.

Not only do I write about these deals, but you can see them all on my YouTube Channel. Just search for InvestFourMore Commercial Rental Properties.

Let's get to it.

2

How I got Into Commercial Real Estate

I grew up in a real estate family. My dad became a real estate agent in 1978 right before I was born. The other day, I saw an agent who remembered me sleeping under my dad's desk while he was working. I was 3. I remember being with him all the time. I thought houses and real estate were amazing. I even drew floor plans on graph paper.

As I got older, I lost the love for real estate, or I simply wanted to do my own thing. In high school, I wanted nothing to do with real estate.

I went to the University of Colorado in Boulder. I started as a civil engineer and then moved into business finance after deciding the high-level math needed for engineering was not for me.

I got through business just fine as low-level math always made sense to me. After I graduated from college, I tried to find a job in finance. I was not even sure what kind of job I wanted, maybe banking or something.

I looked for a job but could not find anything that would pay me what I thought I was worth. I could not really find anything that would pay me anything, but I also do not know how hard I tried.

I went to work for my parents part time. The part-time designation was important to me at the time because it meant my work was temporary and I had much bigger and better things ahead of me.

Those bigger and better things involved real estate. I ended up working full time with my dad and getting my real estate license. I sold houses, and I helped him flip the occasional property as well.

It took me a while to find success in real estate. I am an introvert, and I did not like showing houses to strangers and hated calling people. I managed to make myself do it enough to get by, but I was not burning up the town with all my sales.

I was doing some of the manual labor on the flips to make extra money as well. I would paint some of the houses or install light fixtures. I was cheaper than the contractors we used, and it put some extra money in my pockets as well.

I was able to buy my own house in 2003. I was making okay money, and it was very easy to get a loan back then. I was ecstatic to have my own house, but I had nothing to show for my investments except an IRA with a few thousands dollars in it. I had done really well in investing in stocks during the tech boom and really badly when the market crashed. Funny how that works.

I kept chugging along as an agent and helping my dad flip without making much progress in life.

Then, in 2006, I started to get fed up with where I was going—or more accurately—where I was not going. I decided to make some big changes, so I took on a house flip on my own. My dad helped me buy it, and we still split the profits, but I was to get a bigger share of the profits because I was going to do all the work on the house myself.

I bought a house from the MLS (Multiple Listing Service) that needed a lot of work but seemed like a good deal. I had a friend who was going to help me work on the house. He had more experience than I did with repairing a house. He was not a contractor but had many odd jobs and had helped out contractors with work before.

We started on the house, and things did not go well. First, my friend helped me for about a day, maybe a day and a half, before he decided he had better things to do. I was able to borrow some of his tools, but that was about the only help I was getting from him.

I went to the school of hard knocks. I demolished the kitchen, windows, doors, and even took out a wall. I was not really sure what I was doing, but it was fun for a week or two. Then I had to start putting the house back together. I had done some work like this in the past, and I actually helped a builder frame a house when I was 14 one summer. While it was cool to learn a lot about framing, none of that knowledge helped me on this house.

This was before YouTube, but I did have some contractors I could direct questions to. The trouble was that I was stubborn and tried to do it all on my own without asking for help.

I worked through that house and managed to get the work done in about 6 months! I figured it would take me about a month...maybe longer. I don't know where I got that idea since it would take a contractor and a few guys that long to do all that work, and they know what they are doing.

During that time, I kept telling myself I was saving so much money on labor that it was all worth it. In the end, I didn't make any money because it sold for much less than I thought it would. We were in the middle of the housing crisis, prices were dropping, and my work was not amazing.

The thing that hurt me the most was the opportunity cost. I was not making money as an agent or looking for new houses to flip. I had my worst year by far in real estate and worked the hardest I have ever worked.

I learned that I needed to work smart, not hard. And, at least I had tried something and was not stuck in the same rut I was in before. While it ended up being a colossal disaster, it sent me on a different path.

I worked hard to find my niche in real estate and determine what I loved to do. I loved to flip, but I knew I could not do all the work on properties myself. I thought being an agent was okay, but I honestly did not like talking to people.

Eventually, I found the world of REO. REO stands for real estate owned and is the term banks use for foreclosures they take possession of and sell. I completed one BPO, which is a broker price opinion, for a bank, and I was hooked. I made $50 for completing a report. I did not have to talk to anyone, and all I had to do was take pictures of the home and come up with a value for the bank.

I completed more and more BPOs which lead to me getting REO listings. With the REO listings, I rarely had to talk to people either! Although, the way I got in with the banks in the first place was cold calling them to see how I could list properties for them. While I did not like calling people, I still forced myself to do it.

I was listing houses for more and more banks and asset management companies. I had found my calling, and I was making good money. Now, here is the part where I finally start to talk about rental properties! You were probably wondering when I was going to get to the point.

I was making good money, but I did not have much to show for it, or at least not as much as I thought I should. I knew I had to invest my money better. I could put some money in my IRA and hope it went up in value. I had no control and not much to show for it, even though I maxed out my contributions every year.

I put a lot of time and effort into researching investments. I looked at stocks, bonds, mutual funds, franchises, starting a business, gold, and real estate. I tried to look at everything from an unbiased perspective because I wanted what was best for me. Even though I had been an agent and flipped houses for many years, no one talked about rentals. Or, if someone did mention them, they talked about how horrible they were as an investment.

Over and over, the more research I did, real estate kept coming up as the best investment for me. I wanted something substantial to show for the hard work I was putting in. I did not want to have to wait 30 years to see my accounts grow to a point that I could start to think about retiring.

Rentals had some amazing advantages that the other assets did not:

Leverage: Real estate is one of the easiest investments to get a loan against. Leverage can be risky, but it can also produce much higher returns.

Tax advantages: I was starting to pay a lot of money to the government. If I could decrease the amount I paid to the government and make a good investment, that would be awesome. Real estate offers some amazing tax advantages.

Cash flow: The right rentals make you money every month. You are not simply hoping for them to go up in value.

Appreciation: While I did not have to count on my rentals to increase in value, they certainly could go up in value.

Buying below market value: The other huge advantage real estate offers is you can buy it below market value. I knew this from flipping houses, but I never thought about it much with rentals. I could buy houses at a significant discount and have equity from the very beginning. You did not have to hope prices went up—you could make money right away.

I knew that rentals were the right investment for me. I needed to figure out the right way to buy them.

The other problem I had was rentals could be expensive. I had some money, but as I said, I never seemed to have as much as I should based on how much I was making. Right around this time, my wife and I bought a new house to live in. The first house I bought did not turn out to be a great investment, mostly because I bought it right before the housing crash for full retail value. This time, I would be smarter.

We bought a foreclosure from the public trustee sale, and it was an awesome deal. In fact, other investors were bidding on it to flip it. I borrowed money from my sister and father in law because I had to pay cash at the sale. We paid $210,000 for it. I refinanced it and paid everyone back.

Less than a year later, I refinanced that house again and took out about $50,000 in cash (known as a cash-out refinance). Now I had the money to buy rentals! I did just that, and bought my first rental in 2010 for $97,00. I rented it out for $1,050 a month. It was worth at least $130,000, and I spent $2,500 fixing it up before we rented it out. More on this rental later.

I bought 15 more residential rentals from 2010 to 2015. In 2016, I ran into some problems. The biggest problem was that prices had gone crazy in Colorado. My properties were worth twice what I paid for them, but the rents were only 25% higher. I could no longer cash flow because rents would not cover all the expenses, including the mortgage. You often find this happening in expensive markets.

I took 2016 off and tried to figure out what I would do. I wanted to keep buying rentals. In fact, I set a goal on my blog InvestFourMore.com to purchase 100 rental properties by 2023. I looked at buying in different markets, and I even found a place in Florida that seemed great.

It would take a lot of work to invest in rentals out of state because I would need a new lender, a new agent (I was my own agent in Colorado), a new contractor, and a new property manager. I was working on these things when I discovered commercial real estate.

I had wanted to invest in commercial real estate at some point in my life. I knew there was a need in my area for a certain type of commercial space, and I wanted to buy a big warehouse to fill that need. I had no timeframe for when this would happen or how, but I knew I wanted to at some point. This was not my plan to replace my residential rentals, but it was a dream and fun thing to do in the future.

In the beginning of 2017 when I was still trying to figure out if it was worth investing out of state, I saw an interesting property pop up on the MLS. It was only $110,000, which was half the price of residential properties in the area. I knew that was dirt cheap, which always catches my attention, but then I saw it was zoned for commercial use. I almost didn't open the web page because I didn't want commercial.

Then, I thought I would see what type of property it was. It was a furniture repair store with a shop in the back. It had 3,000 square feet and looked like a steal. I then researched commercial listings and rent. My gut told me this property should rent out for at least $1,500 on the low end. I set up a showing (the commercial agent always has to meet you there on commercial properties). I saw the place, and it was not bad. There was even a partial basement that was not included in the square footage.

I decided to take a chance. At this point, I was flipping from 10 to 30 homes a year, and I had taken over the business from my father. I almost always bought my properties with no inspection, but on this one, I wrote in a five-day inspection contingency because it was commercial and I wanted to verify that what my gut told me was correct.

I sent in a full-price offer the same day the property was listed. The listing agent seemed flabbergasted that I would do that, but we got it under contract. I did not even get an inspection. I researched a few things on commercial and decided it would be incredibly hard to lose on this deal.

It took me 9 months longer to close on this property due to some issues with the seller, but we got it done. By that time, I had bought other commercial rentals as well. We rented it back to the seller for $1,500 a month, and it has been a cash cow ever since—well, until we refinanced it and took $60,000 out above and beyond what I paid for it. I will talk about how that was done later.

I had found my new rental-property investment: commercial real estate. I could buy them below market value and leverage them. They offered great tax advantages, and they generated cash flow when the residential rentals did not.

Now, it was not easy finding deals on commercial real estate. They were not all sitting around waiting for me to buy them, but there were deals. I bought 10 commercial properties between 2017 to 2019 that ranged from 900 to 68,000 square feet. I knew very little about commercial real estate when I started this journey, and I still do not know everything. But, I have learned a lot about how to find deals, finance commercial properties, network, and use cash-out refinances to get my money back out to use again.

3

Start Big or Small?

Many real estate investors start with residential properties, are successful, and move on to something bigger. They invest in apartments or commercial properties. They often sell their residential properties and use 1031 exchanges to buy bigger deals without having to pay capital gains taxes.

Those investors realize that buying bigger deals can often be more profitable and think, "What if I had just started with these bigger deals from the beginning? I would be so much better off."

Many of these investors then tell new investors to skip the small deals and not waste time on single-family homes or small apartments—start with the big stuff first and you will be so much better off.

In theory, I see why they say this because you can make more money with bigger deals and it is easier to scale. However, there are many problems with starting with big deals.

1. To do big deals, you often need a lot more money. If you are using bank financing, you will need 20 or 25% down, which means you will need hundreds of thousands of dollars in some cases. Most investors do not

have $200,000 lying around.

2. You can use partners and other ways to put less money down on investment properties. The bigger the deal, the harder it is to use these strategies without experience. Most people do not want to partner with someone who has never done a deal. It is not impossible, but it is not easy.

3. Believe it or not, it can be hard to get a seller to take you seriously when buying commercial real estate or apartment buildings. When I inquire about a property to the listing agent or the seller directly, one of the first things they ask me is if I have ever bought commercial property. Many people who want to buy apartments and commercial real estate never do. The sellers and agents know this and try to guard their time by only dealing with experienced investors. Is this fair? No, but that is life. If you have no experience, getting your foot in the door can be tough.

4. Many investors also say that buying apartments or commercial buildings is easier because the banks only care about the property, not the investor. I am not sure which banks these investors are working with, but every investor I have worked with wants to know everything about me. They are not looking to loan millions of dollars to anyone off the street just as long as the deal makes sense. A bad investor can screw up the best deal in the world. The more experience you have, the easier it will be to get financing, both from banks and from other sources.

5. Managing and leasing large complexes and buildings is not easy. There is a lot that goes into it, and many property managers aren't familiar with dealing with large projects. There is a decent chance you will have to do the majority of the work on your own. Without experience, this can be a disaster.

I don't want to sound like I am discouraging everyone from investing in commercial real estate. However, starting from scratch in commercial or big apartment deals is not easy. Many investors push "go big or go home." I want people to realize that those investors sometimes have ulterior motives like selling coaching or getting investors to spend their money on their deals instead of investing in real estate themselves.

You can start big from the beginning, but it is not easy, and you usually must have deep pockets. I see many investors saving up for years for these big deals, and I think that could be a mistake.

One of the oldest sayings in real estate is ,"Don't wait to buy real estate, but buy real estate and wait."

There are so many advantages to buying real estate—yes even the smaller deals—that I think investors are making a huge mistake if they are saving up for years to do their first "big" deal. Here is why.

Time works against all of us. We are all getting older and money is always becoming worth less. Inflation means that a dollar next year will buy less than a dollar this year. If you are saving your money, inflation is working against you. If you are investing your money, inflation is working for you, especially in real estate.

I love real estate because there are so many advantages to rentals.

How do you make money with rentals?

Many people will say the stock market is a better investment than rentals because the historical price of stocks has gone up more than the historical price of real estate. However, the price of a home is only a very small fraction of the investment when buying rentals. I love to see my rentals go up in value, but I think of appreciation as a bonus. Here is how a good rental property will make you money.

Cash flow

Cash flow is the income you make after paying all expenses. On a good rental, the rent minus all expenses (including the mortgage) should leave you with income every month. For example:

- Rent is $1,500 a month
- Mortgage, including taxes and insurance, is $900 a month
- Maintenance costs are $150 a month
- Vacancy allowances are $150 a month
- Property management is $150 a month
- The property makes $150 a month

$150 a month may not seem like a lot of money, but that is just one way to make money with rentals. You will also find the rents, mortgage payments, and expenses will vary greatly on each property. Some properties will make more than others, and some will not make any money at all.

Buy below market value

I always get a good deal when I buy rentals. One of the greatest advantages of real estate over other investments is you can buy it below market value. Every property is different. This makes real estate hard to value, and because it is hard to value, that creates opportunities to get great deals. Some sellers want to sell quickly, don't want to make repairs, or don't care about money (sounds crazy, but it happens).

When I buy rentals, I create instant equity by purchasing below market value. Here is an example:

- I bought my first rental for $97,000.
- It needed $5,000 in work to get ready to rent out.
- I fixed it up and rented it out for $1,050 a month.

· After I had fixed it up, I could have sold it for $130,000 to $140,000.

I created instant equity and increased my net worth by $30,000 to $35,000 with one rental. When you get a great deal, it makes investing in real estate much less risky.

Tax advantages

Rental properties offer some amazing tax advantages. Almost all the expenses on a rental are either deductible or can be depreciated. If I get a mortgage on a rental, the interest paid on that mortgage is an expense and is deductible.

The big kicker is that the structure can be depreciated as well. On residential rentals, the structure of a property is depreciated over 27.5 years (39 years with commercial). Using my first rental as an example, the structure was worth $80,000 when I bought it. Every year, I can depreciate $2,909 from my income, which lowers my tax bill. I am not spending this money, and the property is not really losing that value, but I still am able to deduct the depreciation. When I sell a rental, the profits are taxed lower than ordinary income in most cases, and it is possible to complete a 1031 exchange, which defers all the taxes.

Principal pay down

When you have a loan on a property, each payment goes to principal and interest. While we may only be making $150 per month on the rental example I gave above, a couple of hundred dollars is being paid off on the loan every month. Hopefully, you are making much more than $150 a month and are paying down the loans as well.

Appreciation

I do not like to count on appreciation, but that is what most people focus on who are trying to convince you real estate does not offer good returns. Appreciation is great, but I never count on it—it is a bonus to me. It can be a very big bonus in some cases. I bought my first rental in 2010 for $97,000. It is worth almost $300,000 today. Now, to be fair, I am in Colorado, which has had one of the highest-appreciating markets in the country. I would never count on prices going up that high.

One of the best things about rentals is that the value of the property increases with inflation as do the rents. If you have a mortgage, your cash flow greatly outpaces the rate of inflation because you are using leverage. The equity also greatly outpaces inflation because you have less money invested in the property than the property is worth.

If you buy a property for $200,000 with $40,000 down and that property goes up in value 10%, you just made 25% on your money. The property only increased 5% in value, but thanks to leverage, you increased your return five fold. Of course, there may be other costs that came with buying the property, and there will be selling costs, but this is a basic example of how leverage amplifies the returns.

The same goes for rent. If the property is renting for $1,500 a month and the rent goes up 10%, you are now making $1,650 a month. That is not a big deal except that you were making $150 a month before and now you are making $300 a month or maybe $250 if taxes or insurance increase.

On a side note, $150 a month in cash flow is not very much, and I always shoot for $400 a month or more on my properties, but I wanted to use a conservative example. My book *Build a Rental Property Empire* goes into the details of buying smaller rental properties and making the most money you can on them.

Back to my original point: are you better off saving your money until you can buy a big property or investing in small properties first? I think most people are better off investing in small properties first because they are easier to buy, they take less money, are easier to finance, are easier to manage or find a manager for, and they earn you more money than saving.

That last part is the most important part. Even if you find a place to put your savings that will make you 10% a year while you wait, that won't add up very fast. If you have $100,000 and you earn 10% on it, you now have $110,000 after a year. Compounding interest is great, but it takes a long time to really turn into something huge. Real estate can often get you higher returns much faster.

If you take that $100,000 and buy a couple or a few rental properties, you could have:

-$60,000 in instant equity by getting a great deal.

-More than a 10% return on your investment every year with appreciation thanks to that leverage we talked about.

-Cash flow that is coming in every month and could add up to more than 10% of your investment.

-Tax savings thanks to depreciation and interest expenses.

-Principal pay down on the loan.

It seems crazy to some people, but these advantages can more than double your money in a few years or even less. If you are making 10%, it takes you 7 years to double your money.

Not only are you gaining experience, learning about real estate first hand,

and building relationships, but you are also making more money!

What about small commercial properties? What if you want to jump straight into commercial properties but with smaller deals? I think that can work, but it will be a little tougher than owning straight residential rentals. However, with smaller deals, you will need less money, and there is less risk if something goes wrong.

If you feel comfortable with jumping into commercial straight away, remember you don't have to do a million-dollar deal. There are often small commercial properties that many investors overlook. I will talk about some of these properties, which I have bought myself, later.

This also gives you commercial experience, so when you start calling on those big deals, you can say, "Yes! I own commercial real estate."

4

The Basics of Commercial Real Estate

Commercial real estate investing can be very intimidating to those who are learning the business. I bought my first commercial rental property a few years ago, and it took a while to learn all the ins and outs. I had been investing in residential properties for more than a decade before that, which helped me some. There are so many things that are different with commercial real estate. Commercial real estate is complicated, but it also can be very lucrative. You do not have to know everything about the industry in order to be successful either. Once you learn the basics on leases, tenants, cap rates, TI, risk, and lending, you will start to see opportunities and gain confidence. While commercial real estate is complicated, that is a good thing. That means fewer people are willing to venture into the business, which leaves opportunities for the rest of us.

What is commercial real estate?

There are many different types of commercial real estate and even a few different definitions of what commercial real estate is. To me, commercial real estate is a property that is used to run a business, not a property where someone lives. Some people will say large apartment buildings are commercial real estate because you need commercial loans to finance them. However, for the purposes of this section, and in my mind, an apartment building is not commercial real estate. Here are some properties that I would consider commercial:

- Retail stores
- Malls
- Office space
- Storage units
- Warehouses
- Manufacturing facilities
- Gas Stations
- Restaurants
- Bars
- Vacant land zoned for commercial uses

When I think of commercial real estate, I feel anything that the city or county zones as commercial would also be considered commercial. There can also be mixed-use properties that are zoned for both commercial and residential. I own a property with four units where one of the units is commercial and the other three are residential. I consider mixed use as commercial as well since lenders and zoning usually consider them as commercial.

How are commercial rental properties valued?

Residential single-family rentals are often valued based on what similar houses sell for. If a property is rented, it can hurt the value if owner-occupant buyers are willing to pay more than investors. Multifamily residential rentals and commercial rentals are valued based on the income they produce.

The CAP rate is usually what determines how much commercial property is worth. The CAP rate is:

CAP Rate = NOI (net operating income) / Value of the property

If the CAP rate is 10% and the property makes $100,000 a year, the property is worth $1,000,000.

If you can raise the income on a property, you can greatly increase the value. I have done that on a number of my properties. I purchased one commercial rental for $110,000 that did not have a lease in place. It was occupied by the previous owner who said he wanted to leave as soon as it was sold. Once I bought the property, he was not ready to leave, and he ended up renting it back from me for $1,500 a month. I had the property appraised about a year later, and that appraisal came in at $250,000 based on that $1,500 monthly rent and the local CAP rates of 6%.

While determining the values seems like a simple equation, it is not so simple when the property is vacant, needs work, or rented out at below-market prices. That is where the opportunity to increase the income and increase the value comes into play. It is also easy to manipulate the NOI as the seller by not disclosing all the expenses or underestimating the expenses.

How does financing work on commercial real estate?

One big difference between residential and commercial rentals is financing. Most banks will finance residential properties, especially if they have fewer than 5 units. However, many banks do not want to deal with commercial rentals or residential rentals with more than 4 units. The banks that handle commercial loans have a commercial-lending department that deals with these types of properties. That is why many people refer to residential properties that have more than 4 units as "commercial" since they often need financing that comes from banks' commercial sector.

Local banks are often the best banks to offer commercial financing. However, they offer much different terms than they do for personal residences.

Down payment

When you buy a property to live in, you can get loans with as little as 3% down or even $0 with VA or USDA. When buying investment properties, you will need 20% down, and most commercial loans require 25% down. If you want to get into commercial real estate, be prepared for the extra money needed to buy properties!

Loan term

The "loan term" is often referred to as how long a loan lasts. Most people who have 30-year mortgages on their homes have a 30-year term as well. They can keep that loan for 30 years if they want, and as long as they make the payments and adhere to the other loan requirements, the bank can't call that loan due. With commercial financing, there is often a shorter loan term. The loan may only be good for 5, 10, 15, or 20 years, even if the amortization term is longer. The loan term is also called a balloon payment because at the end of the term, the bank can call the entire loan due at that time with one giant payment.

Amortization schedule

The amortization schedule is how the interest and principal portion of the loan payment is calculated. If you have a 30-year amortization, the payments are configured so that all the principal is paid off after 30 years. If you have a 15-year amortization, the loan will be paid off in 15 years. The payments are much higher on a 15-year loan because you are paying it off much more quickly.

You will usually have lower amortization schedules on commercial real estate. I routinely see banks offering 20- or 15-year amortizations. As I said earlier, you may have a 20-year amortization but a 10-year term. The loan can be called due after 10 years, even though it will not be paid off yet.

Rates and fees

Rates and fees on commercial real estate can vary greatly. You will find that some loans will be similar to residential rates, but others can be quite a bit higher. It all depends on the bank, the borrower, the property, and other factors.

Banks also offer adjustable-rate mortgages (ARMs) on commercial loans. There may be a 3, 5, 7, or 10 year fixed-rate period. After that fixed period is up, the rate can increase. You can find ARMs on residential real estate as well, but it is very common on commercial deals.

Most loans also come with origination fees that can vary from .5 to 2% of the loan amount. This fee is primarily how lenders make money. The fee can be higher on commercial loans, but not always.

Appraisals

When you get a loan a residential or commercial property, you will need an appraisal, which helps the bank determine if the property is really worth what the borrower wants to pay or thinks it is worth during a refinance. The appraisals on residential properties typically range from $400 to $800 dollars and can take a couple of weeks to complete. Appraisals on commercial properties can take much longer and be much more expensive! When getting an appraisal on my 68,000-square-foot building, it cost $3,500 and took 7 weeks! We could have gotten an appraisal done faster if we were willing to pay $8,000!

Low-money-down loans

There are options to buy commercial real estate with less money down. You may be able to find a partner or get seller financing. Another option is owner-occupied SBA loans. If your business occupies more than 50% of the property, you may be able to qualify for an SBA loan, which only requires 10 percent down and may even help finance some of the repairs or other costs.

Commercial real estate classes

Commercial property is divided by classes from A through D. Many agents and investors will say a property is A class or B class, which indicates its stability and attractiveness to tenants.

A-class properties are the best of the best and attract the best tenants. They are also the most expensive to rent and the most expensive to buy. A high-end office building that is the nicest in town would be an A-class building. A brand-new Wendy's with a 20-year NNN lease would be considered an A-class property. The big investors look for A-class buildings because they have the best tenants and are the most stable without doing any work.

B-class properties are a step below the A class. Those properties may not be in the best locations, may be older, or may not attract the highest rents, but they are usually still good properties that are rented out or can be rented out fairly quickly. Many of my properties are considered B-class after we stabilize them and have solid renters in place.

C-class properties need some work. They could be vacant, need repairs, or be in a location that is not attractive to most tenants. They also may be rented but run down or be rented for well below market value.

D-class properties are the worst of the worst. They are in areas that see declining population or have other major problems. The properties themselves need significant work or may need to be scraped.

I do not pay attention to which class a property is in most of the time. The definitions are very subjective and can change based on who is using them. If you hear someone talking about classes of buildings, this is what they mean. If you want to describe how I invest, I usually take a C-class building and turn it into a B. That is how you create value.

Finding and buying commercial real estate

I have mentioned a few of the commercial deals I have found, but they were not sitting there for months just waiting for a buyer to come along. It can be tougher to find commercial deals than residential deals. Most residential properties are listed for sale on the MLS, or multiple listing service. If you are looking for a property to buy, you can talk to an agent who has access to the MLS and see 95% of what is for sale.

With commercial real estate, there is no MLS that every property is listed on. Some commercial properties are listed on the MLS; some are listed on Loopnet; some are listed on other websites; and some are not listed anywhere! I bought one of my properties as a pocket listing, which means the listing agent did not market it except for telling me about it. Commercial properties are listed all over the place, and many times, it is not about what you know but who you know. I have been able to get a few deals because of the connections I have in the commercial real estate industry.

Some commercial properties are on the MLS, and you can find deals there, but you have to keep your eyes on other sources and network with local commercial agents.

How to repair commercial real estate

One thing that surprised me when I started investing in commercial real estate was how much it cost to fix everything! I got bids from several commercial contractors, and the costs were incredibly high relative to what I was used to paying for my residential projects. I also saw other businesses paying incredibly high rates for remodels in the commercial space.

I never used any of these commercial contractors. I used my residential guys, who surprisingly, were familiar with commercial standards for construction. There are differences in terms of how commercial properties are rehabbed. You must worry about:

- Fire suppression.
- Different codes for construction.
- ADA accessibility (handicap).
- Parking lots.

Overall, there is not a huge difference between residential and commercial construction. I do bring in subcontractors for some things like sprinkler systems, but my residential guys could handle almost everything else, including roofing, HVAC, electrical, and plumbing. Using residential contractors instead of big commercial specialists saves me a ton of money.

It is smart to make sure you are doing everything to code with commercial real estate. Some businesses may need the city to inspect their places of work, and the city may require building permits for many reasons.

How to lease commercial real estate

The leases on commercial real estate are much different than residential. I prefer the leases on commercial real estate because they are longer and stronger, and the tenants usually pay more expenses.

Length of lease

Most residential leases are one year long, maybe two. You will often see commercial leases that are 3 years, 5 years, or even 10 years or longer! I have a land lease on one of my properties that is 20 years long. Businesses want longer-term leases because they don't want to have to move, and landlords like keeping the same tenants.

Escalation clauses

Some might be thinking, *I don't want a 20-year lease!* Think about how low the rent will be in 20 years compared to market rent due to inflation. That is true, but many commercial leases include escalation clauses that increase the rent every year or every three years. In many of our leases, the rent increases by 3% every year.

Expenses

On single-family rentals, the tenants pay many of the expenses: utilities, lawn maintenance, and snow removal. The landlord still pays for property taxes, insurance, and repairs. On multifamily rentals, landlords often pay for utilities, lawn care, snow removal, and more. On many commercial leases, the tenants pay for almost everything. These are called NNN leases, and the tenant pays all utilities, common area maintenance, insurance, property taxes, management, some repairs, snow removal, lawn care, and more. There are gross and modified gross leases as well where the tenant does not pay all these expenses, but the rent is much higher on those types of leases.

Quality of tenants

I think the quality of tenants is better with commercial real estate. I have some great tenants in my single-family homes, but I have some not-so-great tenants in my cheaper multifamily properties. Commercial tenants are people who own businesses and have some financial acumen. There will always be some bad apples, but overall, my commercial tenants are fantastic because their livelihood depends on the business.

Tenant improvement

One thing that landlords do not have to deal with on residential properties is tenant improvements. On many commercial properties, the landlords will make repairs or customize properties for the tenants. The tenants do not pay for all the remodeling they need. We have spent tens of thousands of dollars on tenant improvement to get more renters into the properties. That money helps increase the value of the properties through higher lease amounts.

What are the risks with commercial real estate?

Up to this point, commercial real estate seems amazing! I think it is amazing, but there are some risks. Commercial real estate is more complicated and has caused a lot of bankruptcies.

Vacancies

It typically takes much longer to lease a commercial property than it does a residential property. Some commercial rentals have sat vacant for years or even decades. Long leases are nice to have, but long vacancies can be horrible for those who are not prepared. When investing in commercial real estate, you must have cash reserves that can cover the expenses during long vacancies.

There are ways to counter the vacancies by offering tenant improvement, breaking up large units into small units, or remodeling.

Economic downturns

People will always need a place to live, but they will not always need a building for their business. During bad economic times, commercial real estate often suffers. There can be more vacancies, and businesses can go bankrupt. Most commercial real estate keeps chugging along, but not all of it.

Business liability

When you rent to businesses, you inherit some of the liability that comes with those businesses. If a business hires someone to remodel their unit but doesn't pay them, the contractor can place a lien not only on the business but also on the building. If a business does not pay sales taxes, that may be levied against the business and the building. If a business gets sued or is doing something illegal, that could cause problems for the owner of the building.

Environmental hazards

Some businesses use or produce things that are not healthy for the environment. They could use oil, gas, chemicals, or produce pollution, toxic waste, or who knows what. Those hazardous materials could damage the property or get the business and property in trouble with the local governments or EPA.

Conclusion

Commercial real estate can be a great investment and has made many millionaires and billionaires. There are risks to investing in commercial real estate, and it is not for everyone. While figuring out all the ins and outs of financing, buying, leasing, and managing commercial rentals is complicated, I think it is well worth the trouble.

We will go into all of these items in more detail later, and we can look at my case studies to see how they apply in real life.

5

Commercial Versus Multifamily

Commercial and residential real estate investments are very different, and learning the ins and outs of each takes time. Commercial real estate may be great, but I think residential real estate is an easier investment to understand. But, if an investor is well versed in commercial and willing to work hard, they can make a lot of money.

Many investors want to invest in multifamily apartment buildings because that is the investment pushed by most gurus. While you can make a lot of money with multifamily, it is not easy.

One of the biggest factors to consider when investing in apartment buildings is many other investors are trying to do the exact same thing, especially on large buildings. Many apartment investors have stopped buying because they feel properties have become overvalued due to all the demand.

There are still deals, and I know investors who are doing very well, but it is not as simple as many make it sound.

There are pros and cons to each type of investment. If we assume we can get the same type of deal on an apartment as we can a strip mall, here are some of the things that make me want the strip mall.

Ease of management

I mentioned earlier that it is tougher to manage and lease commercial real estate. That is true, especially the leasing part, but once you figure it out, it can take less work than large apartment buildings.

In a strip mall, I might have 5 to 10 tenants that occupy 30,000 to 60,000 square feet. Those tenants are on long-term leases, and once they are settled in and pay their rent, they rarely ask for anything. With NNN leases, they also pay for almost everything.

With a 30,000- to 60,000-square-foot apartment building, you might have 30 to 100 units with 30 to 100 different tenants. You are also dealing with tenants who can't afford a property or might not have steady income. Managing all of those tenants is a full-time job, and many large apartments have a full-time manager living at the building. That manager can handle a lot, but that also means you have to hire them and make sure they are doing their job.

You will also have maintenance, vacancy, and utility costs for all of those units. You also may need to slowly remodel those units if you are looking to add value. That means kicking tenants out, remodeling, and renting out one unit at a time.

This can be done, but it can take years and significant work. The commercial property could also have vacant units, but the tenants are usually less of a headache, and once the commercial property is rented out, it usually needs much less management.

Risks

Many people assume there is huge risk with commercial properties, and there can be. If you have a giant single tenant and they leave, you may have a vacant building for years. That is why I stay away from giant single-tenant buildings. I prefer to have my commercial buildings broken up into separate units or smaller, which makes them easier to rent out.

There are also risks with apartment buildings. They can fall into disrepair very quickly with the wrong management or tenants. There can be drug use, crime, or other problems.

I once saw a 50-unit property used as a meth lab. The city shut down the entire building and kicked everyone out because it was not safe for any tenants. The insurance did not cover drug use, and the property went into foreclosure. It took years for a new buyer to come along, and they had to remodel almost the entire place before tenants could move back in again. Apartments do not come without risk.

Financing

Financing is similar with apartments and commercial properties. To be honest, HUD sponsors some great loans for large apartments. Many local and national lenders also prefer prefer residential over commercial. However, commercial financing is available for commercial properties. There are also SBA loans for owner-occupied commercial buildings. Those are low-down-payment loans for business owners or building owners who also operate a business in the building (self storage properties being one example).

Economic

Residential wins if the economy goes down. People will always need a place to live, but not everyone will need to have a commercial business if things go bad. If times are rough, commercial can be rough too, but businesses will still operate, and if you have solid tenants, rents or occupancy may not change at all when things get tough. If you have month-to-month tenants who are hanging on by a thread, you could be in trouble, and leasing out properties in a down economic environment could be tough.

Conclusion

There are risks and rewards to both large apartments and commercial buildings. For me, I love the value-add potential of a great tenant in a commercial property. I can bear the risk, and the ease of management is appealing to me since I can self manage most of the properties with very little work. Leasing commercial properties out is tougher, but you usually need far fewer leases and tenants, and the tenants stay much longer.

6

What Type of Commercial Properties Do I Like?

What are the best types of commercial properties to buy? What is my preference? There are many kinds of commercial investments, from a Wendy's on a 20-year lease to a vacant 250,000-square-foot office and manufacturing facility (I tried to buy one of these once).

Knowing what to look for can be daunting since there are office buildings, retail, restaurants, industrial, land, multi-tenant, and single-tenant buildings. There is even mixed use, which is part commercial and part residential. While there is a lot to consider, I do not limit myself to one type of property over another. I mostly look for a great deal that will cash flow.

Many big commercial investors will look for the A-class tenant who has a long-term lease. Lenders also like to loan on those types of properties. However, there are plenty of loans for other types of properties. Here are the two most-important questions you should ask when considering commercial or any type of rental property:

1. Will the property cash flow after it is stabilized?
2. Can I add a significant amount of value, or is it already a bargain?

Big commercial investors care about stability and a place to store their cash. They are not usually looking for value-add properties that need a lot of work. I am looking for value-add properties that sometimes need a lot of work. Other times, they simply need a new tenant or renegotiated leases.

I also prefer properties that have multiple tenants, at least on the bigger properties. On some of my smaller properties, there is only room for one tenant. I prefer multiple tenants so that if one vacates, I am not stuck with a giant empty building sucking away my resources. Although that can happen on my smaller buildings, I have a few of them, so if one goes vacant, I still have tenants paying rent in the other buildings.

One of my biggest fears about investing in commercial real estate was having a giant property with one tenant that left. After I expanded my thinking, I realized avoiding that scenario was really easy: don't buy big buildings with only one tenant!

My ideal property

I will cover every commercial rental property I own later, and some of my properties fit this description to a tee. Here is my perfect commercial rental property:

-It's large enough for multiple tenants. I think 10,000 to 100,000 square feet is great.

-It's in decent condition. It could be older, but I want the major systems to have been updated within the last 20 years and functioning well.

-It's occupied by rent-paying tenants. It does not have to be 100% occupied, but I would like some tenants so I'm not eating all the costs while we stabilize it.

-It's priced well below market value because the rents are low, there are vacant units, there is some deferred maintenance, or the seller is simply motivated.

-The current rents would at least cover my loan costs while we work on increasing the NOI (net operating income).

I have bought many properties that meet these guidelines, although some are single-tenant buildings. It's okay to buy single-tenant buildings, but know if they go vacant, you could be left paying all the bills.

I don't want to buy the Wendy's with the 20-year lease because it will be priced too high. The owners know they can sell to a big investor looking to park money, and they will ask top dollar. There is no room to increase the value unless the Wendy's will increase the rent they pay, which is highly unlikely since they have a long-term lease. Some rent increases may be built into the lease, but those are probably meant to keep up with inflation and not to add income. There is almost no way to add value unless the market changes how they value the property (CAP rates change), and I do not want be at the whim of the market. I want to make the value increase myself.

Am I looking for industrial, retail, office, or something else? Yes! I am not picky when it comes to property type. In fact, I like having many different types of properties as it gives me some diversification in case one industry is in a downturn.

Many people are scared of retail because popular opinion says everything is moving online. Yes, some things are moving online...but not everything. If you are flexible, properties can have many different uses, not just a clothing store or Radio Shack. Many businesses are looking for retail space. More people also work from home, but the majority still commute to their workplace. There will always be a need for office space and businesses.

I might not suggest buying the giant mall that has been vacant for 20 years because all the retailers left and the mall was only set up for retail, but you could buy the small strip mall, which there always seems to be demand for. Or, you could be creative and convert the giant mall into the most awesome haunted and property and laser tag facility ever created!

Later, I will show you how adding new leases and tenants can greatly increase the value of a property. I want to buy properties that make some money but that can also make a whole lot more money. If they are under leased or have vacant units, they are usually priced well below similar properties that are stabilized and producing market income.

The other great thing about these types of properties is there is not as much competition from other investors. There will be way more investors looking to buy residential properties because those are easier to understand and find.

Big commercial investors will be looking for stabilized properties that are more likely to be solid income producers for years to come without much work. Not as many people are willing to take on the value-add, smaller properties or even know they exist. Most investors are not willing to take on bigger properties either, especially the vacant ones, because most banks will not touch them. That is another reason I like properties that produce some income—it makes them much easier to finance from the beginning.

What about new builds?

I own a property that is in a prime development area, or at least that is what the city thinks. It is in an area I think will be prime for development in the future, but I do not think the area is ready for it yet. It is located on a major highway with over an acre of land.

Many of my YouTube viewers ask me why I am not bulldozing the houses and the commercial building so I can build a new strip mall or other new building. To be honest, I don't like new builds.

The main reason I do not like new builds is it is hard to get a really good deal. It is tough to build a property for less than market value. You need to be a builder who can manage the entire process, which is a job in itself.

I got really excited when I saw the ads for steel buildings that could be put up for $30 a square foot or something. I knew buildings like that were selling for well more than $100 a square foot. Think of how much money I could make if I built these steel buildings, rented them out, and then sold them to big investors.

I started looking into the total cost and learned the $30-a-square-foot deal did not include the land, the utilities, the concrete, the electric, the plumbing, the baths, the HVAC, or even insulation! I was buying a shell, and when I added all those other costs, it was costing me more to build than what I could sell the property for. Now I knew why other investors weren't putting up these buildings left and right.

While I could not build a building for $30 a square foot, I have bought existing buildings for that cheap or cheaper! This is the same reason I flip houses rather than building new ones. I can get a better deal, and it is easier.

Building from scratch is not easy. I saw the process first hand when I worked on a framing crew one summer when I was 14. Technically, I was volunteering because I was too young to work, but I learned a ton. The actual building takes a lot of work because there are so many moving parts, but on top of that, you have to deal with the local governments.

You need to have the land, the right zoning, the permits, the approvals, the inspections, and the final sign offs. With commercial properties, the city's needs and allowances create even more complications. I have seen commercial projects in the works for years before they were approved. I leave those projects for the big investors who have much more time and money than me.

When you buy older properties, you also may get away with more from the city. When you build new properties, they are getting more and more expensive every year because material and labor costs are rising and the the city or county sets more requirements for what each building needs. The city may grandfather in or be more lenient with older buildings that existed before the current codes came into effect.

What about big vacant buildings?

I like buildings where you can add value, but you have to be careful about buildings with too much potential. A huge, completely vacant property could be trouble. Often, there are reasons why these properties sit vacant and no one else touches them. Sometimes the cost to rehab them may be more than what they will be worth once stabilized.

There could be concern about the demand for those buildings once they are rehabbed. There could be environmental concerns or zoning problems. Some big-box stores place zoning restrictions on properties when they build them. If they move out, they will not allow a similar store to occupy the building. If the only use for that building is another box store, it could sit empty for years.

I have been tempted by big vacant buildings because I knew I could create so much value. The problem was it would take so long and cost so much money. In the end, common sense won me over, and I am glad it did.

The other big issue with big projects and new construction is projects that take a very long time leave you more exposed to market changes. The longer a project takes, the riskier it is.

7

Where Should You Buy Commercial Rentals?

Something else that can change the value, risk, and returns from commercial real estate is the market you buy in. I just purchased a property with 25,000 square feet for $230,000. That is not a typo, but I also bought a 68,000-square-foot property for $2,100,000. Guess what—both were great deals.

The properties were in different markets, which made a huge difference regarding their worth. The 68,000-square-foot property is worth twice what I paid for it after we added value through new leases. The 25,000-square-foot property is worth about $250,000 because we haven't done anything to it yet!

How can two properties have such different values?

The properties are 90 miles apart. One is in a town with about 100,000 people in a very popular area with a fantastic economy. The other town has about 11,000 people and is the largest town in the area. The markets are vastly different.

The median home value in the larger town is $320,000, and in the smaller town, it's $177,000. I knew one market very well but didn't know the other as well. I did know enough to know a great deal when I see one.

The replacement value of the 25,000-square-foot property is more than $2,000,000. That in itself does not make it a great deal, but it is part of the puzzle. I did some research on the town to see what the commercial landscape looked like.

How did I do my research? I looked at which commercial properties were currently for sale, and I looked at what commercial properties had recently sold for. I found that this property appeared to be an albatross. It was huge, appeared to be in decent shape, and was dirt cheap.

I decided to take a trip to see what the area was like. I had been in the town many times...but not for years. I took some time driving the commercial areas to see if there were many vacant properties or properties for rent, and I looked for warning signs that the area would be tough to rent in.

I found that most properties were occupied. Only a few were vacant (which every town will have), and they were even building a new commercial property. There were very few for-lease signs as well. I decided that the town had potential for commercial tenants. I also knew that the property was cheap enough that I could make money without getting top dollar for rent.

How do you know what a good market is?

I would have never even considered this market for commercial properties except that a couple of people in my office were in interested in properties there due to the cheaper prices. I happened to find this property when searching the MLS in the area.

It is tough to say what makes a good real estate market because every investor is so different. I like investing locally because I can use my real estate license to save money. I also know the area well and know prices well. Figuring out the market just 90 miles away was a little tricky. I have yet to try to rent out the property, so there could be some serious learning curves on the way.

If you can invest locally, it is a massive advantage. You know the area, and you can drastically reduce the risk. You may live in a very expensive market or a very cheap market, but there are most likely still deals in your area. The property I bought 90 miles away looks like a steal, but it will most likely rent out for much less than a similar property would in my town, and it may take longer to find tenants. It also may be harder to find property management or people to work on the building (if I decide not to send my people that far).

When you invest in a smaller market, there could be more risk because there may be fewer businesses in the area who want to rent space. In larger markets, you could lower the rent or offer incentives to attract businesses. In smaller markets, businesses simply may not be looking for space.

In large markets, the prices will be higher and the returns may be lower because more investors are looking to buy in those areas. With any real estate deal, the returns can be greater on riskier properties.

I would stay away from areas that are losing population or have an influx of vacant properties. Some areas have too many properties for the businesses in the area.

Conclusion

I was good with taking a chance on the property in the smaller town because it was so cheap. I figured I could rent it out for almost nothing and still make money. You still have to be careful with big buildings like this because the insurance and property taxes can be steep. Property maintenance can also take a big chunk of cash if work is needed. The risk was worth it to me. If this had just been an okay or slightly better deal than what I could get locally, there is no way I would have taken the chance.

II

Commercial Numbers, Analysis, and How To

How do you value properties? How do you rent them out, and how do you find the deals?

8

What Makes a Deal a Deal

One of the toughest things to figure out in real estate is what to buy. I mentioned I like to buy many different types of properties, but how do I choose the exact property to buy? That is not easy to answer as every property is so different.

I flip a lot of houses, and I can tell you exactly how I analyze a flip. I usually look for at least 15% profit margin in each flip based on the selling price. If I sell a flip for $200,000, I want to make $30,000, and if I sell it for $300,000, I want to make about $45,000.

I take all the expenses like repairs, carrying costs, selling costs, financing costs, and the unknowns that almost always pop up, and I subtract them from what I think the property will sell for once we are done fixing it up. If the property will sell for $300,000 and my costs are $70,000, I need to buy for $185,000. You need big margins in flips to make money.

While I know how to analyze the flip, in some cases, I may change my profit margin a little because it is an easy or a tough flip. The bigger the repair job, the more profit I need because there is more that can go wrong, and with a small repair, job I may be willing to take less profit because I can get it sold quickly and there are fewer unknowns.

I talk much more about flipping houses in my book *Fix and Flip Your Way to Financial Freedom.*

Rental properties are a little trickier, especially commercial rentals. I always want one thing with every property and that is an awesome deal. I could have flipped and made money from just about every rental property I have purchased. I may not have made my desired 15% profit, but I could have made money because it was an awesome deal.

Many people ask me if it is okay to invest in rentals if they cash flow yet cost full retail value. First, there is no one way to invest that works for everyone, so it is up to you to determine what works for your goals. For me, I want a great deal on every property I buy.

Why do I always want a great deal?

I buy many properties with private money and then refinance into long-term loans. In order to refinance the property and get all of my money back out (and sometimes more), I have to get a great deal. I can usually only refinance 75% of the property's value.

If I buy a property for $100,000, make a few repairs, and rent it out, and the property is only worth $120,000 after we are done, I will only be able to get a $90,000 loan. For some people, that works great and would be a good rental for them. I am greedy. I want great deals. I would want that property to be worth $150,000 or more when I am done. If it was worth $150,000, I could get a loan for $112,500 and get most if not all of my money back out. Then, I can keep reinvesting my money into new properties.

You don't have to buy properties with the goal to refinance them, but I still think it is wise to get a great deal on every property. If the market changes or you need money in the future, the more equity you have, the better. You may want to refinance in the future.

One every property I buy, I want to have at least 30% equity minus any repairs I made based on the purchase price. What does that mean?

If I buy for $200,000, I want the property to be worth $280,000 if it needs $20,000 in work: $60,000 ($200,000 x 30%) + $20,000. I actually want much more, but that is the bare minimum with commercial. Renting out commercial properties can take longer, and they can be riskier, which means I want a lot of upside.

How much cash flow do I want?

I don't just want a good deal on my rentals—I also want to make money every month. The reason I stopped buying residential rentals is that I could no longer make money with them even if I got an awesome deal. The price-to-rent ratio was too low and the expenses too high.

I used to buy residential rentals that had an 8% to 10 % CAP rate (more on CAP rates soon), but now rentals are at a 6% CAP rate, so I'm getting a great deal! It is not easy, but I can still buy commercial properties that have an 8% CAP rate or higher. Sometimes they are vacant or need work, but they are out there. It is very hard to get those numbers with residential properties, even with multifamily in my market.

When buying commercial rentals, or any rental, I want at least an 8% CAP rate based on the price I pay. That means I make 8% on my money if I were to buy the property with cash. I want to make more than 8% in reality, and I do that by using financing, but that CAP rate helps me figure out what a good deal is. Again, 8% is the minimum, and I prefer 9% or 10% which I have been able to get on most of my properties.

Remember, these are my rules and won't work for everyone, but they do work for me.

I avoid extreme risk

I can find properties that meet these criteria and still will not work for me. Why? They are too risky. It is hard to analyze what that means, but big, vacant buildings are risky. Buildings that need tons of work are risky. Buildings that may take years to rent out are risky.

A good rule of thumb is:

If you can't wrap your head around how much work a project will need or how long it will take to stabilize, don't do it!

That is, unless you have a ton of cash and are willing to risk not seeing any return for years on that cash.

I have been tempted by high-profit deals and even had a few under contract to buy. I have canceled a few high risk deals after we couldn't get together on price or the repairs seemed to be too much. After canceling the deal and thinking about it, I am almost always glad I did not do the deal.

How do I weed out deals?

One thing I look at first when analyzing a deal is the price per square foot. I look at that because I have an idea of how much a property will rent out for based on the square footage. That is how most people determine rent prices on commercial property.

If I see the price per square foot is below a certain level, I know to look further into the deal. $100 per square foot or lower is a pretty good deal here, but I don't have rock-solid rules that I never break. I will go over that for the right property, but most of the time, that number is a good indication I should dive in deeper.

Conclusion

Knowing exactly which deals work or do not work isn't easy. With my rentals, I want to be very picky because I will most likely own them a long time. I have some guidelines they must meet, but in reality, they almost always exceed those guidelines, and I know they are great deals. If I have to question how good of a deal they are, they are usually not worth doing.

9

What Is the CAP Rate, and Why Is It So Important?

If you have researched investment properties, you have probably heard of the CAP rate. CAP is short for "capitalization" and is often used to determine the value of income-producing real estate. The CAP rate is a measure of what the returns will be assuming you pay cash for a property. The CAP rate will not give you the returns when you have loans on properties, but it will give you an idea of what a property is worth.

InvestFourMore Cap Rate Calculator (https://investfourmore.com/calculators/cap-rate-calculator/)

If you are involved in commercial real estate, understanding CAP rates and how they work is vital, as is knowing what CAP rates are in your area. CAP rates can be used to trick people into thinking a property is a better deal than it is. Plus, incorrectly figured CAP rates can provide amazing opportunities for investors.

What is a CAP rate?

The CAP rate is a common figure used to determine the value of a commercial rental property. If you buy a property for $1,000,000 and it generates income of $70,000 (7% return) a year, the CAP rate is 7%. If the property generates $100,000 a year, the CAP rate is 10%.

Is CAP rate used for the value or purchase price?

The CAP rate can be used to determine the value of a property, the return from the property, and many other factors. It can be used to determine what a property is worth if you already own the property. For example:

- I own a property that is making $100,000 a year. The market CAP rates for that property are 10%, so the property is worth $1,000,000.

When a property is for sale, the CAP rate is given based on the asking price and income.

- If someone needs to sell fast, maybe they advertise the above property for $909,000 as an 11 CAP. Or, if they are willing to wait for the right buyer, they list it at $1,100,000 and 9 CAP.

I could also buy the property for $1,000,000 when it makes $100,000 but add $20,000 in income. I bought the property as a 10 CAP, but after improving the income, it is now a 12 CAP based off the purchase price. I can say the property is a 12 CAP based on what I paid, or the property is worth $1,200,000 based on a 10 CAP now. Either way, both statements would be true.

Why CAP rates are important to real estate investors.

CAP rates are important because that is how most commercial properties are valued and advertised. If you want to invest in commercial real estate, knowing CAP rates, how they are determined, how they can be manipulated, and how they can make you money is important. Depending on your situation, they may not be the best way to judge how much money you are making.

I think cash flow or cash-on-cash returns are more important indicators on a rental property. Cash flow tells you exactly how much money you are going to make including expenses and debt service. The cash-on-cash return will tell you what percentage you are making on the money you have invested, which is much more important to me than CAP rates.

The CAP rate is valuable as a tool to value properties and tell you what you should pay for properties, but it only tells you the return if you are paying cash. I prefer to leverage my money, so the CAP rate is not the best indicator of how much money I will make.

How do you calculate the CAP rate?

The higher the CAP rate, the more money the property makes based off the purchase price or the value.

The CAP rate calculation is very simple:

CAP Rate = Net operating income divided by the price of a property.

The CAP rate can be figured out very easily, but the tricky part is knowing how accurate the income numbers are on a particular property. The net operating income is used to determine the CAP rate, and that number can be easily manipulated.

Factors that affect the CAP rate

The net operating income, or NOI, is the money the rental property will make after accounting for expenses. Debt service is not included, but property management, taxes, insurance, maintenance, and other expenses should be included. The NOI can easily be manipulated because different investors will use different expense numbers. Some investors will include allowances for vacancies and maintenance, while others will not. If a property is self managed, the landlord may not include any expenses for property management. Make sure not to blindly trust NOI figures given to you!

You will find different investors include different expenses to determine the NOI. Some investors may include vacancies and property management, and others may not. Some investors may not include any maintenance in their NOI projections to make their properties appear more profitable. If you are basing a purchase decision on the cap rate, you need to make sure all expenses are accounted for. If the total rent for a property is $10,000 a year and the NOI is $10,000, there are obviously expenses being left out of the equation unless it is a true triple net property. An NNN lease is when the tenants pay all of the expenses. Although, even with an NNN lease, there are usually some additional expenses.

Here are other expenses that should be included:

- Property taxes
- Property insurance
- Property management fees
- Utilities paid by the landlord
- Ongoing maintenance paid by the landlord
- Vacancies
- Expected maintenance expenses
- HOA fees
- Any onsite management

· Tenant Improvements

Can you trust the CAP rate?

If the expenses and NOI are not calculated correctly, it may show an inflated value based on market CAP rates. The higher the NOI is with the same CAP rate, the higher the value will be. It is easy to manipulate the CAP rate by fudging the NOI.

I never trust the numbers given to me by a seller or agent. I am not saying they always intentionally give bad numbers, but they might, or they may not even know how to determine the correct numbers. I verify the numbers with what I think the expenses should be, and I also try to see the actual expenses the seller pays. In most commercial transactions, the seller should be willing to give out those numbers, although they may require interested parties to sign a nondisclosure agreement, which means the interested parties cannot share those numbers.

What is a good CAP rate?

Knowing what a good CAP rate is isn't easy. The CAP rate is relative to many other factors, like the location, the condition, and the property's use. The condition and tenant also affect whether or not the CAP rate can be considered good. I personally want to see at least a 9 CAP on the properties I buy. These could be vacant properties or properties that need some work. After they are leased and repaired, I want at least a 9 CAP depending on how much work is needed. Properties actually sell at a 7 CAP or lower in my market, so I know I am in good shape and will be creating a lot of value by purchasing properties that will be a 9 CAP based on what I paid.

CAP rates in different areas of the country

Another tricky thing with CAP rates is they are not the same everywhere. The market determines what the CAP rate will be, and it varies greatly in different areas. In hot markets like Los Angeles, CAP rates may be as low as 4%, while markets in the Midwest may see CAP rates of more than 10%. Different cap rates can change the value of properties by hundreds of thousands or millions of dollars.

For example:

- NOI: $100,000 a year with a CAP rate of 4% equates to a value of $2,500,000
- NOI: $100,000 a year with a CAP rate of 10% equates to a value of $1,00,000

The CAP rate varies based on demand in the area, how stable the economy is, and what returns investors expect. Investors are willing to make less money in California relative to the cost of a property because they feel there is more upside for rent increases and rent appreciation. In areas with less-stable economies, rents may not go up or could even decrease. Higher risk means the landlords must make more money to make a purchase worthwhile.

CAP rates vary based on the type of tenant and building

CAP rates will vary in different locations or in the same location based on the tenant and the property. In my area, Northern Colorado, the CAP rate could be 5 or 6% on long-term tenants like a Wendy's with a 20-year lease. The CAP rate rises to 7 or 8% for less-stable tenants who may only have 1-year leases. If a property is vacant, the CAP rates rise as well because the owner must spend money and time finding a new tenant, and they will not be collecting rent during that process.

New markets and CAP rates

CAP rates can also help you figure out what a good market is for investing. You may be able to tell if a market is worth looking into based on the CAP rates. If you are looking to make the most money you can on the money you invest, you want a high CAP rate. If you are looking for long-term plays that may have high appreciation, you may want low CAP rates.

While common sense says that you will make more money with a high CAP rate, there are also reasons why CAP rates are high. The higher the CAP rate, the more risk. The market, the property, the tenant, or another factor may be very risky, causing that high CAP rate. Some people are okay with risk. Others are not.

How to add value to commercial properties

I have bought a number of commercial properties that were good deals for a variety of reasons:

- They were vacant
- They needed repairs
- They were under rented
- They were not marketed well

Most people considering weren't considering these properties because something was wrong with them. The CAP rates showed what the value was, but the CAP rates also created an opportunity. If you can buy a property at a 7 CAP and raise the income, you can greatly increase its value.

For example:

- A property that makes $100,000 a year at a 7 CAP is worth $1,428,571
- A property that makes $150,000 a year at a 7 CAP is worth $2,142,857

$50,000 is $4,166 a month. By increasing the income on a property by just over $4,000 a month, we have increased the value by $700,000!

There are a number of ways to increase income. You can raise rents, manage the property better, increase the NNN, lease out a vacant unit, etc. On one of my properties, we have increased the value by about $2 million by adding two tenants and raising rents.

When not to use a CAP rate

If you want to know the exact return on a property, the CAP rate may not be the right tool. If you are using a loan of any kind, the CAP rate will not help you at all. If you are making repairs or improvements, the CAP rate will not tell you what return you are getting on that money. The CAP rate can be a piece of the puzzle to let you know what the property will be worth, but there are many other numbers to look at.

Conclusion

The CAP rate and NOI can be used to help determine the returns on rental properties, but there are also many other factors to consider, like the cash flow and cash-on-cash returns. When looking at CAP rates, make sure the numbers are correct! They could be off in your favor or against you. When you understand how CAP rates work and use them to your advantage, you make a lot of money.

10

How to Find Deals on Commercial Real Estate

One of the most important parts of commercial real estate is finding the deals, at least for me. Certain huge, institutional investors will buy at full market value and simply want a small yield, but that is not how I invest.

I want to get fantastic deals that also provide the opportunity to add value. You can find commercial real estate for sale in many areas, and most of those listings are set at full retail price, but luckily, not all of them are. One reason I love commercial real estate is there is less competition, meaning more deals are in plain site. It is still not easy, but it can be easier than looking for residential deals.

Some of the easy places to look are:

MLS

The Multiple Listing Service is where most houses are listed. However, some commercial properties are also listed on the MLS. Often, a residential agent will list commercial properties on the MLS because that is the only place they know to put it. Many commercial agents are also very good at their jobs and list properties everywhere they can, which includes the MLS. Do not discount the MLS just because it contains mostly residential properties.

Looking through my MLS right now, I see 114 commercial properties for sale in my county alone! I have gotten many deals from the MLS even when I was not looking for commercial.

The first commercial property I made an offer on was on the MLS. It was an amazing deal at $110,000. It was a furniture-restoration business that had been in operation for decades. The owner of the building also owned the business and was planning to sell the building and move his business to another location. The building had a retail front on a somewhat busy street and a workshop in back with about 3,000 square feet total.

I made a full-price offer the same day it was listed, and I think I surprised the listing agent. Commercial agents tend to do things a little more slowly than residential agents. I ended up buying the property after a few months waiting for some liens to clear up. We then rented it back to the furniture-store owner for $1,500 a month with the owner paying most of the expenses. I later refinanced that property, and the appraisal came in at $250,000. I was able to take more than $50,000 in cash out of the property.

This deal was on the MLS waiting for anyone to buy it. What I have found is that there are not nearly as many buyers for commercial properties as there are for residential properties. I find deals for residential flips on the MLS as well. In most cases, those houses have a ton of competition. However, with commercial real estate, I am often the only one making an offer.

These deals are not always available on the MLS, but they do show up. I have bought four properties from the MLS, and a few of them were just sitting on the market for months. Because of how long they were listed, I was able to make lower offers and get a great deal.

Loopnet

This is the most popular commercial-listing service, but it does not have every property, and they limit the listings the public can view. Only the listings that the agents pay for are available for everyone to see.

There are still deals on Loopnet. It is a little tougher to find those deals because Loopnet has some issues. As I said, they do not show the general public every property that is for sale. The agents must pay to get their listings seen by everyone. If they do not pay, only agents or brokers like myself have access to every property on the site.

I spent more than $300 a month to get access to all of the listings on Loopnet. I have found some properties that were available to everyone publicly and some properties that were only available to those who pay every month.

While I get really annoyed at Loopnet for charging me so much just to view listings, some agents only use Loopnet to list their properties. In one case, I knew of a property that had been listed in the past. It had been priced well, but the listing was expired. I called the old listing agent and asked if the property was still for sale. He said he would check, got back to me in a few days, and apologized that it wasn't listed anymore. I needed to contact the sellers directly.

I looked up the sellers, who happened to be in Texas. I am in Colorado. I asked them about the property. I was able to find the real-estate division of this large corporate company and ask if the property was still for sale. To my surprise, they said it was for sale and listed with an agent.

I looked up the agent and texted him, and he replied it was on Loopnet.

However, since he was not paying for a premium listing, I could not see the property on my basic public search. There was no sign on the property and really no way to see it was for sale unless you had the Loopnet premium service that showed all listings.

That is why I paid for the premium membership, even though I feel like I am getting shafted.

Commercial Real Estate Agents

My best deal was through another commercial real estate agent. I was a residential agent and knew I did not know quite enough about commercial real estate to go at it alone. I decided to enlist the help of a commercial real estate broker. I would be losing out on the commission as the buyers, but I thought it was worth it.

This choice turned out to be more than worth it since that agent found me an amazing deal! He let me know first about a property he was selling. If I had not been working him, there is no way he would have sent that deal to me. Honestly, I was very lucky he had that deal, but he was one of the most well-known agents in the area.

Networking is one of the best ways to find deals in the commercial real estate world. The reason networking is so important is you never know where or if a property will be listed. It may be on Loopnet, the MLS, Craigslist, Facebook, or nowhere. There may be a sign in the window...or no sign at all. It could be the agent knows of a property they are going to list, but it's not listed yet.

I have hosted a monthly commercial broker meeting at my office a few times, and it has always been well worth it. At every meeting, the brokers network and talk about any deals they have coming up. Often, these deals are not listed and won't be listed for quite some time. Agents from the meeting have also talked to me afterwards and mentioned deals they may be getting or deals that other agents may be getting. They know that I am willing to let them represent me as my agent if they bring me a decent deal!

Networking is one of the best ways to find deals and rental properties.

Off Market

Off-market properties are out there. Some owners are willing to sell, but they have not yet taken the steps to list their property. They have been thinking of selling or waiting for that perfect time, but they have not started the process. You can sometimes reach those sellers via direct marketing.

To be honest, I have not bought any properties from my direct marketing yet. However, I have bought off-market properties. My very first commercial deal was from a friend who was looking to get rid of his commercial shop. He knew I was an agent, and I mentioned I might be willing to buy the property directly.

We worked out a price, and the property has been a great investment. I will discuss all the details on that deal in may case-studies section.

I have sent out letters to commercial property owners and gotten some great responses. However, we never were able to make a deal work for multiple reasons. One response was from the owner of a strip club, and that was not my cup of tea. I think my wife may have killed me if I bought that. Another property was just leased at a rate that was simply too low for the asking price. Other properties were not quite what I was looking for, but close.

We have been in talks with other commercial sellers. We have also asked different sellers about drive-for-dollar deals, which involves driving around looking for ugly properties. Many people do this for residential properties, but you can also do it for commercial properties. When you drive for dollars, you drive around or look for properties as you drive to other locations that are vacant, need work, or have other signs they may be distressed. When you find those properties, you send them a letter, knock on their door, or find another way to call them and see if they want to sell.

FSBO

I also bought a property from Facebook Marketplace. One of my contractors told me about it. It was really cheap—like really, really cheap. The seller told me I was competing with many other buyers. It was an amazing deal, and it has been a great property.

There are many ways to find FSBO (For Sale By Owner). Many owners want to sell their properties, but not with an agent. They don't want to pay the real estate commissions, or they simply do not like real estate agents. You can find FSBOs all over:

- Facebook
- Craigslist
- Yard Signs
- Newspapers
- Local publications
- Networking

Conclusion

There are so many ways to find deals on commercial real estate. Keeping track of them all can be tough, but the good news is few people are looking that hard. Many commercial listings also take a while to sell. I am not trying to encourage people to be lazy, but you don't always have to act as fast or be on top of things as quickly with commercial real estate as you do with residential real estate.

11

Financing Commercial Real Estate

Commercial financing can be used for more than just commercial property. Commercial loans are also available for residential properties. When a residential property has more than four units, many say you need a commercial loan because traditional residential stop lending if the property contains more than that. While commercial lending can be used for residential or commercial properties, most banks treat these properties differently.

Getting a loan on residential properties, no matter how many units there are, can be much easier than getting a loan on straight commercial properties. When I've tried to finance or refinance my commercial rentals, many lenders flat out said they do not have any commercial loan programs—even on a property that only has one, tiny 44-square-foot commercial unit and three larger residential units.

Lenders that do loan on commercial properties often offer different programs than they do for residential properties. A local lender I have used for many of my residential properties gave me 5- or 7-year ARMs on my residential properties with 30 year amortizations yet would only give me 15-year fixed loans on the commercial properties.

If you are confused by these terms, do not worry—determining loan terms can be tricky. Here are some financing-term definitions:

Amortization

This is how long the loan will last if the minimum payments are made until the entire loan is paid off. If you get a 30-year loan and make the minimum payments, you would pay the loan off in 30 years. 15-year loans follow the same principle. The shorter the loan term, the higher your payments are because you are paying more towards the principal every month.

Term or Balloon

This is how long the loan is guaranteed to last. A loan can have a 30-year amortization but only a 10-year term. The payments are based on a 30-year payoff schedule, but the loan can be called due by the bank after 10 years.

Points or origination fee

These are charged by most lenders and is usually how the lender gets paid. A point is a percentage of the loan amount that is usually paid when the loan is first taken out. If the lender charges 3 points, they are charging 3%, which can amount to big dollars on high-loan amounts.

ARM or variable rate

ARM stands for Adjustable Rate Mortgage and means the interest rate on the loan can change after a certain amount of time. You will often see a fixed-rate period of 3, 5, 7, or 10 years. The interest rate stays the same for the fixed-rate period and may go up or down afterward.

Prepayment penalty

Some loans will have prepayment penalties. This is a fee you're assessed if you pay off the loan early. There may be a prepayment period of 5 years. If you pay off the loan in 3 years because you sell the property, refinance, or win the lottery, you might have to pay a fee for each month you pay it off early. Prepayment penalties are structured many different ways, but they are usually prorated for how soon you pay it off compared to the prepayment penalty term length.

Non Recourse

This means the loan is only against the business or the property. The individuals who own the businesses or land cannot be held liable for the loan.

Loan to value

This is the loan amount compared to the price of the property. If the loan to value is 75%, the bank will lend 75% of the value of the property, which is usually determined by an appraisal.

Real world example of a commercial loan

Here is an example of the first loan on my strip mall:

- 20 year amortization
- 10 year term
- 7 year ARM with no prepayment penalty
- 75% loan to value
- 4.6% interest rate with a .5% origination fee

The payment is calculated based on paying off the loan in 20 years. The loan can be called due in 10 years, and the interest rate is fixed for the first 7 years.

Loan terms can greatly affect the payment amount, rate, and the risk. My loan had a payment (principal and interest) of $10,050 based on the $1,575,000 loan amount and $2,100,000 purchase price. The amortization greatly affects your monthly payment amount. If the amortization had been 25 years, the payment would have been $8,844. Likewise, a 30-year amortization would cost $8,074 a month. By contrast, the payment on a 15-year amortization would have been $12,129.

- 15 year loan: $12,129
- 20 year loan: $10,049
- 25 year loan: $8,844
- 30 year loan: $8,074

You will have much more cash flow with a longer amortization, but it takes longer to pay off the loan. You also will usually have a higher interest rate. The rate may be 5% if you choose the 25 year amortization, which would actually make the payment $9,207.

I will not get into this much in this book, but my preference is to increase the cash flow with longer loan amounts even if the rates are a little higher. I prefer to take that extra cash flow and invest it into more real estate that will make me 15% or more of pay off a 4 or 5% loan.

The origination fee on that loan was $7,850, which was .5% of the loan amount of $1,575,000.

Difference between residential and commercial loans

Most of my residential loans had 30 year amortizations and 30 year terms. As long as I make my payments the loan will be good until it is paid off. Most people loans people get on owner-occupied houses function the same. There are 30 year fixed or ARMs, but even ARMs often have 30-year terms.

Additionally, commercial real estate will almost always have a balloon payment. 30-year-fixed loans exist, but they are rare. One consideration of investing in commercial properties is you may have to refinance them in 5 or 10 years when that term is up.

One of the biggest concerns of the last housing crash was commercial lending was drying up. Many people were afraid it would be impossible for thousands of businesses to refinance their loans when they came due. This could cause an economic collapse, and it's one of the main reasons for the bank bailout by the federal government—to keep commercial lending alive!

The lending is also different on multifamily residential properties. Many banks love to finance multifamily residential but not commercial properties. Government HUD loans are also available on large multifamily properties. These have lower down payments than the typical 20 or 25 % most banks will require.

SBA Commercial loans

The government also offers special financing on commercial properties. SBA loans (Small Business Association) loans have lower down payments and may even finance repairs. There are reserved for small businesses only that will occupy the property. The business must occupy at least 50% of the building to qualify.

These loans come with down payments as low as 10% and amortizations as long as 25 years. The loans are a mix of government and local-bank funding, and rates can vary greatly but are usually competitive with regular commercial loan rates.

To be an owner occupant, you do not have to physically be in the building like you would with an owner-occupied home loan. You have to own the business that occupied most of the building. Many self-storage operators use SBA loans because the same person who owns the building owns the self storage business.

Qualifying for a commercial loan

Now that we know a little about how commercial loans work, how easy is getting one? Just like with all real estate, the answer to that is "it depends." It depends on the property, the borrower, and the bank.

Many investors will tell you the bank does not care about the borrower when they lend on commercial properties, only the property. I am not sure which bank(s) these investors are working with, but I have never found that to be the case. Every bank and lender I have talked to cares a great deal about the borrower and their financial position, which makes sense.

The bank wants to lend on great properties, but they don't want to own those properties. The foreclosure process is messy, and most banks lose a lot of money when going through that process. They want a good property and a good borrower.

When I apply for a loan for a commercial property, the lenders want to know my credit score, my debt-to-income ratio, my personal financial statement, and they want to see my tax returns. In fact, with all the properties I have and all the loans I have, I have been turned down before. They have told me my debt-to-income ratio was too low or I had too much going on.

If you have bad credit, no job, or a bad debt-to-income ratio, you may not be able to get a commercial or residential loan.

Banks also like investors who have experience with commercial real estate. If I try to buy a $500,000 commercial property but have never invested in real estate before, they may not want to loan to me, even if my financials are perfect.

They may not want to lend on a vacant building or a property that needs work even if you have experience and a perfect financial position. Getting financing on real estate can be tricky no matter what type of property you are investing in.

It can be easier if you are buying smaller commercial properties. The smaller the deal, the more lenient the bank will be because they have less to lose.

What type of bank should you use?

I have used local banks for all of my commercial-property loans. They have been the easiest to work with and the most affordable. Local banks are also familiar with the local market and the real estate they are loaning on.

I go over the financing I use in the case-study section later in the book, but I have seen rates lower than 5% on commercial loans with 1 point or less origination fee. I have looked into using national lenders and brokers, but the rates have not been much better, and the origination fees have been more than double or higher in many cases.

It does not hurt to shop around, but in my experience, local banks have been the best option for me.

12

Commercial Appraisals

When you get a loan on a property, whether residential or commercial, most lenders will require an appraisal, which is a report that assigns a value to the property and tells the lender the property is worth what you're paying for it. If the appraisal comes in lower than the contract price or the appraiser requires repairs, it can kill a deal and cause a lot of frustration. Appraisals and the guidelines appraisers must follow can also be very confusing.

Why do banks require appraisals?

Banks and mortgage companies love to lend money on property because it is a more-secure debt than cars or businesses. If the borrower defaults on a property, the bank can foreclose on it and take possession. However, foreclosures are not cheap after you factor in paying the attorneys, selling costs, and lost interest. To reduce the amount of money a bank loses from foreclosures, they want to lend money to qualified buyers and make sure any property they lend on is worth what the borrower is paying.

If banks did not confirm values, the borrower could buy a property for much more than it is worth. If the property was foreclosed on, the bank would not only lose money on lost interest, selling costs, and attorneys fees, but they would also have to sell it for much less than they thought it was worth (assuming prices did not decline since the loan was closed).

Paying much more than a property is worth might seem crazy, but it happened all the time before the housing crash. Buyers would pay too much for a property, get a loan, then default on the loan. They usually knew the seller or even were the seller through different corporations. This was obvious loan fraud, but it happened, usually with the help of fake appraisals.

An appraisal is only done by a licensed appraiser.

What is an appraisal?

I used to complete many broker price opinions (BPOs) as a real estate agent, but a BPO is not an appraisal and is not as detailed. BPOs are used to determine market value for banks who may be trying to complete a short sale or for banks who need to know the value of properties that are going into foreclosure or have been foreclosed. BPOs are usually not used to determine property values for new loans.

To complete an appraisal, the appraiser will view the entire property, take pictures, measure the property, inspect the condition of the property, and complete a report that values the property. The report consists of sold comparables, which are properties that have sold recently and are the most similar to the property being appraised (subject property). The appraiser has certain guidelines they follow regarding the comparables that are used to value a property. Sold comps for properties should:

- Have sold in the last six months.
- Have above-ground square feet within 20 percent of the subject.
- Have similar basements (finished or unfinished if applicable).
- Have been built within a certain time frame of the subject (usually ten years).
- Be in a similar condition as the subject.

- Have a similar bedroom and bath count.
- Be in the same neighborhood or within a certain distance of the subject (usually one mile).

If there are not enough sold comparables to meet all these guidelines, the appraiser can expand their criteria and make adjustments. If a property is in a rural area, the appraiser may have to look within ten miles of the subject for comps or look for properties within 20 years of age because there are no other comps. When an appraiser makes adjustments, they will add or subtract value from the comparable properties.

For commercial properties, the guidelines are not as strict for sold comparables because completing most appraisals would be impossible. There are fewer sold commercial properties, and they vary greatly in size and use. The appraiser will try to find sold comparables but will also use the income approach to get a value. The income approach uses the CAP rate and NOI to come up with a value for the property. The appraiser has a lot of leeway for how they come up with the NOI and cap rate, and that can be frustrating.

I go over one of these scenarios on the InvestFourMore YouTube channel. Just search for appraisal and InvestFourMore.

How much does an appraisal cost?

Appraisal costs can vary based on the location, the loan type, and the property type. Here is a very general list of guidelines:

- Single-family homes: $400 to $800
- 2- to 4-unit multifamily homes: $600 to $1,000
- Large multifamily properties: $1,000 to $10,000
- Commercial properties: $1,000 to $10,000

There is no set price, and the price varies based on the size and complexity of the property. I own a 68,000-square-foot strip mall, and we recently needed an appraisal for a refinance. Our lender gave us two bids. The first was to be completed within 3 weeks for $8,000 and the second within 6 weeks for $3,000. We were not in a hurry, so we took the cheaper option.

The cost can also vary based on location and the current demand for appraisals. I am trying to get a smaller commercial appraisal done now, and the cost is $4,500!

How long does it take to get an appraisal?

This varies greatly. In Colorado, we had a shortage of appraisers and a very hot real estate market. It was taking 3 to 4 weeks to get an appraisal completed, which slowed down the buying and selling process. In a normal market with enough appraisers, it should take from 1 to 2 weeks. Again, the more complicated the property, the longer it will take.

For commercial properties, it can take at least a few weeks if not a few months. The problem is commercial appraisers must be licensed for commercial properties, and there are far fewer commercially qualified appraisers. An appraiser must apprentice with another appraiser before becoming licensed on their own. To become a commercial appraiser, it takes more hours of apprenticeship, and it must be with a commercial appraiser.

Who pays for the appraisal?

Anyone can order an appraisal on their own and pay for it at any time. I would not suggest sellers getting an appraisal on their own because good real estate agents will do it for free and are usually more accurate—that is, unless the seller is looking to refinance the property and the bank is requiring an appraisal.

When refinancing a property, the property owner will pay for the appraisal 98% of the time. A few lenders may pay for appraisals, but it is very, very rare. It is also important for the bank doing the refinance to order the appraisal. The bank may not accept an owner-ordered appraisal or even an appraisal that another bank ordered.

During the transaction, the buyer usually pays for the appraisal. The buyer's lender will order the appraisal and pay the appraiser, but if the deal falls apart, the lender may require the buyer to pay them back for the appraisal cost. In some cases, the buyer may be able to ask the seller to pay for closing costs, and that money could pay for the appraisal.

How do appraisal adjustments work?

When an appraiser uses comparables that are different from the subject, they must subtract or add value to the comp. If a comparable sold for $150,000 but is superior to the subject by $10,000, the comparable value would be $160,000. In the report, the $160,000 adjusted value of the comparable would indicate the subject property is worth $160,000.

To come up with adjustments, the appraiser will compare the important characteristics of the subject and comparable sales (at least three comp sales are usually used). If the subject has 3 bedrooms and the comparable has 4 bedrooms, the appraiser may deduct $4,000 from the comparable because it is superior to the subject. If the comparable's characteristic were inferior to the subject, the adjustment would be positive.

Below is an example of some adjustments that might be used by an appraiser:
  Subject Comparable Adjustment to Comp
  1,500 square feet 1,700 square feet -$6,000
  3 bedrooms 4 bedrooms -$3,000
  2 baths 3 baths -$2,500

2-car attached garage 1 car attached garage $4,000

1,000-sq-ft unfinished basement no basement $7,500

Built 1979 Built in 1988 – $5,000

Total adjustment -$5,000

If this comparable home had sold for $150,000, the adjusted sales price used to value the subject would be $145,000. The appraiser would then do the same thing with at least two more sales comps and come up with a value for the subject using these values.

The same thing would be done with commercial appraisals, but more emphasis would be put on the location, use, and condition.

Do appraisers use active comps?

One frustrating aspect of appraisals is appraisers will primarily use sold comps to value a property. Sold comps must be used because you can list your property for whatever price you want, but you won't know what it is worth until it sells. If an appraiser used active comps to value homes, the value could vary greatly based on if the asking price is close to what the home is really worth. An appraiser may use an active comp once in a while if there are very few comps available to help justify value. The active comp is used to supplement the sold comps...not to be the primary focus.

The problem with only using sold comparables is that in a rising market, comps that are 6 months old may not show the actual value of the subject property because prices have risen since then. It is tough for an appraiser to follow an increasing market because they are always using properties that previously sold. If the market is changing fast, those properties won't reflect current prices.

In theory, the appraiser can say the property is in an appreciating market and make adjustments for that, but that almost never happens in real life. I am in Colorado, which has had one of the highest-appreciating markets in the country, and I have seen 2 out of 100 appraisals say we are in an appreciating market. Appraisers do not want to give any indication they are valuing a property too high, and they usually err on the low side.

What happens if an appraisal comes in lower than value?

Banks want the appraisal to come in at or above the contract price to confirm the value of the home they are lending on. Banks will lend on many different loan-to-value ratios. Some loans, like VA, require zero down, while others like conventional investor loans will require 20 or 25 percent down. The bank will base the loan-to-value ratio on the lower of the contract price or the appraisal. If the contract price is $100,000 but the appraisal comes in at $90,000, the bank would base the loan amount on $90,000, not $100,000. In this scenario, with a 20 percent down payment, the loan amount would be $72,000 instead of $80,000. With no money down, the loan amount would be $90,000 instead of $100,000.

As you can see, the appraised value can both greatly affect many buyers' ability to buy a home and the money they need to purchase one. Low appraisals have killed many deals when the buyer was not willing to bring more money to closing or the seller was not willing to lower the price.

The same thing can happen for refinances. When you refinance a property, the appraiser has no contract price. They can ask the owner what the owner thinks it is worth, but the appraiser is mostly coming up with a value out of thin air. The appraiser is pressured not to come in high on values because of the loan fraud we talked about previously. After the housing crash, all the appraisal rules were changed to combat loan fraud, and that makes appraisers very cautious.

I always expect a refinance appraisal to come in lower than I think the property is worth. That is just how the world works.

Why are appraisal guidelines so strict?

Much of the housing crisis was caused by inflated values, and some of those values were high due to lender fraud. In my town of Greeley, Colorado, we had a few instances of fraud. Here is one scenario:

- The builder constructs a home.
- The Realtor for the builder finds an unknowing buyer and promises low payments ($500 on a $250,000 purchase).
- The Realtor, builder, and lender all convince the buyer to use a risky ARM loan where payments will more than triple in one year (often, the buyer does not know how much more the payment will be).
- They all sell the home for at least 20 percent more than it is worth, and the buyer agrees because of the low payment.
- The appraiser is in on the fraud too and inflates his appraisal to confirm the value.

In a couple of cases like this, hundreds of homes went through foreclosure, and many people went to jail. In order to stop this type of fraud from happening again, appraisers were scrutinized for any values that may appear high. A few things appraisers learned to avoid in appraisals to avoid scrutiny are:

- Mentioning a rising market for prices because this could justify higher values.
- Coming up with a value higher than any sold comps.
- Using active comps to value a home higher.

Basically, anything that could be a judgment call to raise appraisal values is avoided by appraisers because they don't want to be investigated for fraud. This makes it tough on buyers, especially in a rising market, because the sold comps may not be as high as their contract price.

Can an appraisal require repairs to be made?

A low appraisal value can mess up a property sale, but an appraisal can also call out needed repairs. On most loans, the lender will require a home to be in livable condition. That means all the major systems must work or be in good condition: plumbing, heating, electrical, roof, sewer. The appraiser will also make sure there is nothing dangerous like peeling paint (could be lead-based paint and poisonous), holes in the walls or floors, broken windows, or mold.

If you are trying to sell or buy a property that has any of these issues, the appraiser may require them to be repaired before closing. The seller could have the items repaired, or in some cases, the buyer may be willing to make the repairs before closing (on REO and HUD homes, it is usually not an option for the buyer to make repairs). If the seller can't or won't make repairs, the deal will usually die and the property will have to be sold with a loan that does not require repairs or for cash.

Unlike an inspection, the seller cannot simply agree to lower the price in lieu of making the repairs. The lender and appraiser will require the repairs be made before closing unless the repairs can be put in escrow.

How a low appraisal cost me $14,000

This is a story about a single-family home, but it shows what can happen with any type of appraisal.

I bought a property flip for $140,250 and had it under contract to sell for $222,500. Even though this property was the cheapest property for sale in its town, the appraisal came in at $208,000. We did our best to help the appraiser come in at value, and we challenged the appraisal with the lender, but none of it did any good. Not only did the appraiser cost me over $14,000, but we found out during the buyer's inspection that the sewer line needed to be replaced, and that cost another $5,300. What should have been a profit of

$35,000 turned into a profit of less than $20,000. It was not my best flip, but I still made money, even with the problems that came up.

Why didn't I put this property back on the market and go for a new buyer?

$14,000 is a lot of money to leave on the table, but I decided to lower the price and continue with the sale. There are a number of factors I considered when deciding whether I should put this home back on the market:

- The buyers were using an FHA USDA loan, which meant they put no money down. Because it was an FHA loan, if I sold to any other FHA buyers in the next 6 months, they would also use the same low-appraised value. I would have to sell the property to a conventional buyer, which shrinks my buyer pool.
- When you put a home back on the market, buyers wonder what happened. I would have to tell buyers that the appraisal came in low, and even if the low value did not bother buyers, they would have to worry about their appraisal coming in low as well. The low appraisal could cause me to get a lower offer price if I put the home back on the market.
- By canceling this contract and trying to find a new buyer, I would have to hold the property at least one more month and most likely longer. It costs quite a bit of money to hold flips since I have to pay taxes, insurance, and mortgage payments. With my financing on this property, it would cost me about $1,500 a month to hold it.
- I had 19 flips going at once when this happened, and I have to sell properties quickly to handle that many properties. If I only had one flip going, I might try to get a new buyer, but for me, I wanted to sell this property and focus on other projects.

There is a chance I could have made more money by putting the home back on the market, but there is also a chance I would not. I would have to find a conventional buyer who was not bothered by the low appraisal, and who offered enough to make up for the carrying costs. It made more sense for me to sell the property faster and not risk the time it would take to find a new buyer.

Did I challenge the appraisal?

We tried to challenge the appraisal, but the appraiser would not budge on his price. You have to ask the lender to challenge the appraisal, and they need a good reason to make the request. They also require more comparable properties, that were not used in the original report, to present to the appraiser. One problem with this property was that it was in a small town and there were few sold-comparable properties available. The appraiser used 5 sold comps, and all of them had sold over 5 months prior to the appraisal. In Colorado, we have one of the highest-appreciating markets in the country, and prices change fast in 5 months. Prices in the area have been rising 10 to 20 percent a year.

Unfortunately, this appraiser said we were in a stable market and did not make any adjustments for using old comps. We tried to argue that fact, provided three new comps that were not used, and hoped the appraiser would come up in value. He did not. He said the comps we sent could not be used because they had basements, and the property we were selling did not have a basement (I guess it did not matter that two of the comps he used had basements). He did not even provide an answer to why he said we were in a stable market.

How can you prevent low appraisals?

As a real estate agent, I have to deal with low appraisals all the time. I've received low appraisals on many of the properties and commercial properties I sell. However, we have made many changes over the last couple of years that have helped reduce the number of low appraisals we see.

Give the appraiser comps to use

I was skeptical about doing this because I did not know if it was ethical or legal. When I do Broker Price Opinions for banks, I am not allowed to take comparable sold properties from the listing agent or anyone involved in the transaction.

However, the real estate commission in Colorado recommends agents provide comps for appraisers. When we see an appraisal is scheduled, we provide as many similar sold properties as we can. I tell the appraiser they are welcome to use these if they would like, but I never pressure them into using my comps. I make sure the comps support the value on our contract, and if there are any abnormalities (distance from property, square feet, etc), I explain in detail why I chose those properties. Most appraisers are very grateful, and this has helped values come in much higher.

We tell the appraiser about repairs

This lets the appraiser know the home may be in better condition than other similar sales in the area. It also helps to justify the price on flips I complete when I sell it for much more than I bought it for.

Be prompt when returning calls or emails from the appraiser

I try to be as professional as possible with all appraisers. I don't want to give them any reason to get annoyed at me or the property. If the appraiser calls or emails me, I will reply as soon as I can. If the utilities have to be on, I make sure they are on or explain why they can't be turned on so the appraiser does not have to make multiple trips back to the property.

Make sure the property is clean and looks great

First impressions mean a lot to anyone. If your property is completely remodeled but has junk all over or is dirty and cluttered, the appraiser may miss all the remodeling work. Present the property to the appraiser like you would a regular buyer.

If you treat the appraiser right and give them comps that help justify the value, you will have much more success getting appraisals to come in at value. If you are not an agent, make sure your agent is doing these things for you.

How can you challenge a low appraisal?

Even after sending in comps, some appraisals still come in low. If an appraisal comes in at less than the contract value, you can ask the lender to challenge the appraisal. Usually, there has to be something wrong with the appraisal, and you need some really good comps to prove the value should be higher. I had a VA appraisal done on a property for some buyers. The appraisal came in $7,000 low on a newly constructed home. Luckily, there were some major flaws with the report, and we were able to get the appraisal raised.

- The appraiser used a property that was 16 years old and over 2 miles away from the subject.
- The appraiser used a property that was 11 years old and over 1.5 miles away from the subject.

The property that was being appraised was brand new and in a suburban area with many new construction sold comparables in the same neighborhood. I have no idea why the appraiser used these comps when so many other properties had sold in the same neighborhood in the last six months. I provided six comps that were very similar to the subject in price, age, and location. The lender challenged the appraisal using those comps.

There is no guarantee the appraiser or appraisal management company will change the value, even with gross errors in a report, but it is worth a try. I have received other appraisals with worse values that were not changed, and on one occasion, an appraiser raised his value by $30,000 after we sent him comps. On this particular deal, the appraisal was not brought up to the full contract price, but the value was raised $3,000, and the seller agreed to lower the price to make it work for the buyers.

When you challenge an appraisal, you (or your real estate agent) have to be able to provide comps that clearly support value and are superior to the comps used in the appraisal. Or, you have to find incorrect facts in the appraisal. If the appraiser said the subject only had a one-car garage and it had a two-car garage, that is a fact that can be challenged.

If a low appraisal comes in, don't rely on the lender to look it over and decide if they want to challenge it. You should look it over, or if you are not a real estate agent, have your agent look it over closely. Look for any incorrect facts or anything wrong with the comps used. Was distance too far, age of the sale too old, square footage off, or a finished basement not included? In some cases, the value is just low and there isn't much you can do about it.

The appraisal came in low on one of my commercial properties, and the lender thought it was a great report. I had to pester him for weeks to give me details on how the appraiser came up with his income numbers for the property.

The lender finally showed me the numbers (they were not in the appraisal), and the appraiser had used the interest from the loan as an expenses on the building. Remember how we talked about cap rate and NOI earlier? Well, the interest on a loan should never be used as an expense when valuing a property. That was a major error, and once I pointed it out, the appraisal was revised almost $500,000 higher.

If you want to challenge an appraisal, here are the steps to take:

- Get the appraisal from the lender
- Review the appraisal for errors
- Review the comps used in the appraisal
- Point out any errors made to the lender
- Give the lender at least three better comps to use for value

With those tools, the lender should be able to challenge the appraisal and give you a fighting chance.

Conclusion

If you have appraisal issues, don't give up hope. I know many lenders will not pursue these avenues unless they are asked. Many real estate agents will not pursue these options either because they don't know they exist. In some cases, there is nothing you can do about a low appraisal or one that requires repairs, but it doesn't hurt to try to get the value raised. Remember, appraisal requirements are limited to owner occupants. Many investor loans will have the same repair and value requirements as well.

13

How to Find Tenants and Manage Properties

Finding tenants for residential properties is not terribly difficult and, usually, a quick process. You determine market rent, place an add on Craigslist or Zillow, and wait for the calls to come in. In some areas, you may have to use a real estate agent, but that is rare.

Finding tenants for commercial rental properties is completely different. It is possible to find a tenant on Zillow or Craigslist, but it is not as likely and will most likely take much longer.

If you have a smaller property that appeals to mom-and-pop businesses, you may have better luck with regular advertising channels as well, but the bigger and more complicated the property is, the harder it will be to rent out.

I have had a very easy time renting some of my commercial properties and an extremely tough time renting others. I decided to fix up my first commercial property a little before we put it up for lease. The property had about 3,500 square feet on the main floor, and it had a full basement. The basement was unfinished, and we decided to try to rent out the main floor and leave the basement as it was. We painted, replaced the flooring, put in a little kitchen, and made some other repairs.

As we were repairing the property, a company approach us asking if it was for rent. I could not believe it! We actually ended up renting the property to that company for what we were asking. We did not even have to put a sign up.

While renting out that property was easy, some of my other commercial rentals have been much tougher. My 68,000-square-foot commercial rental property had two vacant units in it when I bought it. One of the units had been vacant for 7 years. The other had only been vacant for about a year.

The unit that had been vacant for 7 years was not being marketed very well, and I thought that was the reason no tenants had been found. We ended up putting my new real estate brokerage in that unit and tried to rent out the other unit.

I thought we would find a tenant fairly quickly because we tried to lease it for a little less market rent. I put the property on the MLS, Craigslist, and Facebook, and we did not find any interested tenants...except for one. The agent who had tried to rent it out before had a laundromat that wanted to rent the space, but they wanted at least $200,000 in tenant improvements. They wanted to lease the space for even less than we were asking, and it would have taken almost ten years for us to make our money back through rent for what the tenant finishes would cost.

I did not think that was a good deal for us, so I held out. Eventually, we started to get more interest in the property. I hosted a commercial brokers meeting, and I was allowed to present a few properties to the group since I hosted the meeting.

I only had one property for rent, and it was that commercial space. I told everyone about the space, and one of the brokers knew of a tenant who was looking for a space to lease.

A dance studio that had leased the same space for 30 years in the basement of a city building. They wanted a new space but had not found anything, or maybe they had not looked very seriously.

We came agreement with the dance studio for a 3-year lease after completing $40,000 in tenant improvements. Ironically, potential tenant became interested at the same time. They wanted to start an event center but had never run that type of business, needed more tenants improvements, and wanted to pay less rent. Renting to the dance studio was a no-brainer.

What I learned from this experience is that it is not always how well you market with commercial real estate but who you know!

I see other commercial spaces marketed many different ways. I have seen large properties advertised with just a sign, in Loopnet, in the local MLS, or seemingly not listed for lease anywhere! When I lease out a property now, I always advertise multiple ways.

Loopnet

Loopnet is a commercial listing site for sales and leases. Most commercial real estate agents know to look for properties on Loopnet. However, using it is not simple. I can list a property on Loopnet for free, but only agents with a Costar membership will see the free listings. I recently obtained one of those memberships, and it costs more than $300 a month.

Not every agent is willing to pay that kind of money for the Costar/Loopnet membership. If you want everyone to see the listing, you have to pay a fee, which varies from $79 to a few hundred dollars depending on how much you want done. I would suggest paying the fee to ensure everyone can see the listing.

You can also use CREXI, which is like Loopnet but cheaper and contains fewer properties. Other commercial listing sites have disappeared over the years, and a few, like 42 Floors and Ten-X, are still around.

MLS

I also list my properties for rent in the local MLS system because agents will look there as well. Commercial agents may not be looking on the MLS, but residential agents will, and many residential agents will know the occasional commercial tenant. Those agents may not know where to look for places to lease, so if you are on the MLS, it can be very advantageous.

Craigslist

Craigslist has started to charge for some listings, but it is only $5. While not as many people search Craigslist as they used to, it is still worth listing properties on there. We have also found deals on properties for sale on Craigslist.

Facebook

Facebook has taken some of the business away from Craigslist. The Facebook marketplace is getting more and more popular. I even bought one of my commercial properties from Facebook marketplace. Our local MLS lists some of our properties on the MLS automatically, and we get a ton of inquires on some of our properties.

Signage

We put signs on all of our properties that are available for lease. We have had some fairly large signs and banners made so they are easy to see.

Networking

If I have a property available for lease, I mention it to all the commercial agents I know. If there is a networking event, I attend and see if I can mention it there. These events are also great for learning about properties for sale or for rent.

Social Media

Advertising your property on your own social media pages doesn't hurt. You may have friends or family who are looking for a place to rent or know of someone looking for a place. A simple post on Facebook can do wonders.

What about real estate agent commissions?

Something that can surprise new commercial real estate investors is having to pay a real estate agent who represents the tenants when they lease a property. The agent contacted me on the first rental I leased. I had to pay him 3 percent of the entire lease amount for the entire lease term.

The lease amount was $4,500 a month for three years, which is $162,000. I owed the agent $4,860 as soon as we signed the lease! If you are marketing on the MLS, Loopnet, or to other agents, be prepared to pay them.

Some agents are looking to get 3.5 or even 4% of the lease amount as a commission. The commission is always negotiable. Some agents will look to get paid in other ways, such as $1 per square foot for each year of the least. That can add up to even more money depending on the property and length of the lease.

How long can it take to rent out vacant spaces?

One of the biggest risks of owning commercial real estate is the length of time units can sit vacant. The bigger the space, the longer it can take. Many people, including myself, shied away shy away from commercial rentals because of that. No one wants a 60,000-square-foot building sitting vacant for three years.

When I dove into commercial real estate, I realized there are ways to mitigate this risk.

I try to avoid massive commercial properties with one tenant. This poses the biggest risk to me. I have one 52,000-square-foot unit, which is a grocery store, in my 68,000-square-foot building. It's large, but it is not the only unit in the building. I have other tenants that can help offset the losses if the grocery store were to go out of business.

I also have strategies for large spaces. The larger the space, the harder it is to rent out. The rental rates are usually lower, too. If I am willing to spend some money to break a large space into smaller spaces, I can charge more rent and lease spaces out faster and more easily.

I have plenty of cash reserves in case a space goes vacant. You can make a lot of money with commercial real estate by buying value-add properties and either selling them or refinancing them. Do not spend all of that money. Save it for a rainy day or a vacant commercial unit.

How do you determine what to charge for rent?

Determining rent on commercial properties is tougher than on residential properties because every property is different, and there are usually far fewer properties for rent. You will also find a wide range of asking prices.

If you belong to Costar, you can see what some places rent for, but again, you will find wide ranges for what seem like similar properties. You will also see different prices for different types of rentals. A gross lease will rent for much more than an NNN lease because the gross lease includes more costs that the landlord pays.

If you look on Loopnet, the MLS or can find commercial properties listed elsewhere, you can see what other landlords are charging. Sometimes, those landlords are asking market rates, and sometimes, they are dreaming! Some landlords want to rent out properties right away, and some don't mind waiting years for the right lease.

One of the hardest parts of commercial real estate is figuring out how much to ask for the properties. A good commercial agent can help, but I would not rely solely on them. I personally look at all the asking prices, which is usually based on price per square foot, and assume my properties will rent on the lower end.

How does price per square foot work?

Many people get confused when they see a property listed for $10 a square foot. Some people even see that and think the property is renting for $10 a month! Yes, common sense is not always common.

A $10-per-square-foot rental rate means the property rent is $10 per square foot per year. If the property is 1,000 square feet, it will rent out for $10,000 a year, or $833 a month.

What kind of business should you lease to?

A space in one of our buildings garnered interest from multiple tenants. Sometimes, finding tenants is easy, but not always. These were the interested tenants:

- A laundromat
- A dance studio
- An event center

The laundromat wanted more than $200,000 in tenant improvements paid for by the landlord, which we were not willing to do. That knocked them out of the running, but there were other reasons we did not like them:

- A laundromat might not attract the right crowd for other businesses in the building
- There might not be a need for another laundromat in our area

- They did not have a long track record of success with other laundromats
- A laundromat could damage the building due to humidity

The dance studio was an ideal tenant because they:

- Had been in business for 30 years.
- Wanted minimal tenant finishes.
- Were easy to work with and pleasant.
- Fit in with the rest of the tenants in the building.

The event center was risky because:

- The owners had never operated an event center.
- They wanted a liquor license, which brings in more risk and hoops to jump through.
- They were not pleasant to work with and jumped around with different agents and representation.

We chose the dance studio because we wanted a solid tenant that would be easy to work with. The dance studio has been great, and it looks like they will be in business for a long time. The other business were a much higher risk and were higher maintenance.

You can't always choose the perfect tenant, but you have to be careful who you rent to. You need to check credit, history, financials, and much more to see if that tenant is a good fit for your building.

How to manage commercial rental properties

Managing commercial properties is easier in many cases than managing residential properties. The leasing is the tough part. Most commercial tenants are self sufficient and do not need hand holding or constant attention. With NNN leases, the tenant takes care of and maintains their space for the most part.

The management part comes in with collecting rent, but that is usually easier as well. In many areas, it is easier to evict a commercial tenant, and they know if they want to stay in business, they have to pay their rent.

You also must maintain the property that the tenant is not responsible for. Lawn maintenance, snow removal, and trash cleanup all have to be set up. Once these things are set up with the right people, there is not much else to think about.

You also must keep track of the accounting and the NNN costs. The NNN costs can go up or down based on the actual costs to the landlord. Many landlords keep the NNN the same while their expenses go up. You have to stay on those costs and update the tenants on those costs.

A few companies that will handle the leasing process for you, but they may not handle management. You may have trouble finding a full-service management company that will do both.

Conclusion

Renting out commercial properties is the toughest part of the business—and the riskiest as well. In down economies, finding tenants can be difficult, and you have to make sure you find the right tenants. Landlords often spend a lot of money on tenant finishes, and they don't want to spend $50,000 on a property only to have the tenant go out of business a year later.

14

How does Tenant Improvement (TI) work?

While I was looking into the strip mall, the listing agent mentioned TI. I was newer to the commercial real estate game after spending most of my time in the residential world. I did not feel too bad because, after meeting with the listing agent, my partner asked me what TI was. I told him it must be taxes and insurance. I was wrong. TI stands for Tenant Improvements and describes repairs made to a unit for the tenant. The improvements may be paid for by the tenant, landlord, or a combination of both.

What does TI consist of?

TI may consist of anything the tenant needs for them to operate their business. The building we bought had a restaurant that moved in a few years prior to our purchase. The owner of the building agreed to pay for $150,000 of tenant improvements prior to the restaurant moving in. The restaurant owner managed the improvements, but the landlord paid for them.

The improvements consisted of new kitchen equipment, paint, flooring, a new floor plan, and more. TI can consist of just about anything the tenant needs. In another unit, we constructed two new rooms for a dance studio, painted the walls, opened up the ceiling, and added windows. We paid for those improvements, and they added the finishing touches.

Why would the owner pay for tenant improvements?

Many people assume that tenants pay for the improvements when they rent a space. However, many owners are willing to fix up their buildings for tenants. While it might seem crazy to spend $150,000 for a restaurant to lease a space for 5 years, it makes sense when you dig into the numbers.

- The tenant paid more than $6,000 a month for their lease. That is $72,000 a year.
- It would take a little over 2 years for the owner to get their money back after making those repairs.

The owner of the building is making about a 50% return on their investment by leasing that space to the restaurant assuming no one else would rent it. The decision to spend that much money on tenant improvements gets trickier when you may be able to lease out the space but for a lower rent or short lease time. If you could rent it out for $4,000 a month without doing any work, it takes more than 6 years to make your money back.

Can TI increase the value of the property?

Tenant improvements can make it easier to lease space out and raise the rent on a space. The only benefit to raising the rent is not only that you make more money every month, but you also increase the value of the property.

TI value-add case study

The property we bought was sold at about a 9 CAP (9% CAP rate). I think the CAP rates in my area for this type of property are closer to 7% for market value, but we got a really good deal. How much did the restaurant lease add to the value of the property?

- $6,000 a month x 12 months = $72,000 a year in added income.

- At a 9% CAP rate, $72,000 a year adds $800,000 in value.
- At a 7% CAP rate, $72,000 a year adds $1,028,571.

The reason landlords or owners will pay for tenant improvements is not just because improvements will increase the rent; it is also because they increase the value of their properties. If they are looking to sell or refinance the property, a sold long-term tenant can add millions of dollars to the value.

If we consider the tenant who was only going to pay $4,000 a month in rent and did not require any tenant improvements, that lease would look like this:

- At a 9% CAP rate, $48,000 a year would add $533,333 in value.
- At a 7% CAP rate, $48,000 a year would add $685,714.

While the lower-dollar lease is adding value to the property, it is adding hundreds of thousands of dollars less in value.

How can tenant improvements add value outside of leases?

Tenant improvements offer multiple ways to add value to a property. We already talked about how they can add value with increased rents and how those rents will not only bring in more money but increase the value of the building. Tenant improvements can add value in other ways as well.

When you make tenant improvements, you are improving the building as well as the tenant's unit. If you make the right improvements, it will be easier to rent out the units in the future if the current tenants leave. When the owner spent $150,000 for the restaurant, he made that space much more appealing for any business, especially another restaurant. Another restaurant may need a few things changed, but they most likely will not want to spend that much money again. It also may be much easier to rent out the space when it is already set up for a restaurant.

On the other hand, if you make improvements that are very specific to one business, you may make it harder to rent the space to another tenant. If you finish a space for a bowling alley, you may not be getting any of your investment back if the bowling alley leaves unless you can find another bowling alley to rent the space!

Who should pay for TI?

Another consideration is who should pay for the TI and how. In most cases, the TI is paid for by the tenant, at least in part. The tenant could pay for the costs up front; they could pay for the costs by increasing their rent for a certain amount of time; or they could simply pay for the costs by paying more rent than another tenant who would not require as much tenant improvements.

While many people think it makes sense for the tenant to pay for the improvements since it is their business, it actually makes more sense for the landlord to pay for it if the landlord wants the highest value they can get for their property. For example:

- The tenant pays $3,000 a month in rent, and the tenant pays $50,000 for TI.
- The tenant pays $4,000 a month in rent, and the landlord pays for the $50,000 in TI.

In scenario 1, the tenant pays lower rent but has to front the $50,000. One of the biggest issues is many tenants may not be able to front that money on top of everything else they will need to get their business running. Even if they have all the cash in the world, it takes them 50 months to break even. Up until that 50th month, they have paid more in rent and TI than if the landlord paid for the TI and the tenant paid higher rent.

In the second scenario, the tenant pays more rent, but they need less upfront cash. The landlord has to front more money for repairs, but they have a much more valuable building with the higher lease. In the first scenario, the building is worth $514,285 assuming this is a NNN lease. In the second scenario with higher rent, the building is worth $685,714.

In my opinion, it makes sense for the landlord to pay for most of the TI if they can increase the rent to make up for it. Not only does the landlord make more money in the long run from increased rents, but the value of the property also increases from the day the lease is signed with the higher rents. The value of the property increases much more than the costs of the TI in most cases.

If the landlord decided to refinance the property with a loan at a 75% loan-to-value ratio, they could get a loan for $385,713 with scenario 1 or $514,285 with scenario 2. They could get much more cash back if that is their goal.

Will commercial tenants stay longer with more tenant improvements?

Some of the best tenants will require quite a bit of TI. They will want their space to cater to exactly what they need, and it may be tough for them to find landlords who are willing to spend money on TI. If they can find a commercial property owner who will spend money on TI for them, they may be more likely to stay in that space for the long haul.

The more expensive the TI is, the more likely that tenant is to stay in that space. It is tough to find a landlord who will spend tens of thousands of dollars on TI, and once they are in a space, they will tend to stay there. By spending money on TI, the landlord can attract better and longer-term tenants.

Conclusion

TI can be expensive for the tenant or the landlord. The landlord usually has more to gain by attracting tenants who will pay more rent and stay longer, and the value of their property will increase if they are able to charge higher monthly rent. Before we rented out one of our vacant spaces to the dance studio, a potential tenant wanted to start a laundromat in that unit. They wanted at least $150,000 in tenant improvements made before they would consider the unit. I thought that was crazy because it would take ten years to make that money back based on the price they wanted to pay. However, that lease would have added almost $400,000 in value to the property. It could have made sense to spend that much if we had no other interested tenants. However, that dance studio lease added more value because they were willing to pay a higher lease rate and only needed $40,000 in TI.

While completing TI for tenants often makes sense, the landlord can pick and choose the right tenant and the right TI to complete. Had we converted the space for a laundromat and they went under, there would be very few tenants who would want that space without major renovations, and we would have wasted a lot of money.

15

Commercial Leases

An NNN lease is very common in commercial real estate. I have used them on the commercial rentals that I own and on commercial spaces that I have leased. NNN stands for net, net, net and is often called a "triple net lease." It means that the tenant pays most of the expenses. They pay the rent, fees, property taxes, property insurance, and CAM, or common area maintenance. NNN fees are added onto the base rental fee, which is usually calculated as a dollar-per-square-foot number like $15. There is some confusion regarding what is covered on an NNN lease, but this is what I have seen as an investor/broker who owns and rents out commercial spaces.

What expenses does the NNN lease include?

Common area maintenance (CAM)

When I first heard the term common area maintenance, I was thinking of a common area for many businesses, like a reception room or hallway. The CAM does include areas like that but also includes many more areas! Here are things that are often included in the CAM:

- Roof
- Parking Lot

- HVAC
- Exterior maintenance
- Utilities for the building
- Landscaping
- Signage
- Snow removal
- Security
- HOA fees

Often, even property management and accounting costs are the responsibility of the tenants to pay in a NNN lease.

What does the NNN lease not include?

While it seems like every expense is included in an NNN lease, there are some expenses that are the responsibility of the landlord or a particular tenant. For my strip mall, we have spent money on renovating vacant spaces for new tenants.

The money we spent fixing up an individual unit is not counted as CAM. If we paint the interior, add some walls, or remodel a bathroom, that is the landlord's or that particular tenant's responsibility. The work done on an individual tenant's space is often referred to as TI, or tenant improvements. On our building, we agreed to pay for some of the repairs, and the tenant agreed to pay for other improvements.

When we painted the exterior of the building and made the entire property look nicer, that could be considered an NNN cost. Capital expenses may or may not be included in the CAM depending on the lease.

The landlord usually cannot charge the tenants for their own business expenses that are not directly related to the building, any debt that the landlord takes on, any late fees the landlord accrues for missing payments, or something that happened due to landlord negligence.

It is important to know each lease is different, and commercial leases can be very long and complicated. It is wise to have a professional review the lease for you to make sure it says what you think it says.

How are NNN lease rates calculated

The landlord determines what the NNN lease rates are, but they must be based on real expenses. The landlord cannot make up whatever they want and make the tenants pay it. In most leases, the NNN cost calculation, including when they are calculated and how that information is delivered to the tenants, is outlined.

On our lease, the landlord must calculate the expenses and send a report to the tenants every year. NNN costs are estimated at the beginning of the lease, but they can go up or down based on the actual expenses accrued. When we took over the building, the tenants were paying NNN costs of $1.50 a square foot. That rate was well below what the actual costs were for the building. The total cost is closer to $2.50 a square foot.

To reach that number, the landlord should calculate all the fixed expenses that are included in the NNN lease and maintenance costs for the building. They may also be able to charge some capital expenses based on the lease.

NNN lease versus an absolute lease

Commercial real estate can be confusing! There is a lot of opportunity in the business but also a lot to learn. One of the many confusing parts of commercial real estate is different opinions about what certain terms mean.

For example, some people will say that none of the capital expenses are included in an NNN lease, only an absolute lease. It is hard for me to come to grips with this as most of the triple net leases I have seen include some form of capital expenses. I don't know if these NNN leases are created incorrectly or the definition has become muddled over the years.

One of our tenants even has an NNN lease where they are not only responsible for all the costs on their unit, but they also pay them and arrange for all the repairs and maintenance! Your best bet is to read the lease and make sure you know what it says, not assume that an NNN lease is the same in every case.

Can NNN lease rates change?

One tricky part with NNN leases is that you cannot predict exactly what the expenses will be. Snow removal could be needed one time in one year or ten times the next year. The management—and many other—costs could increase.

The triple net costs are not usually set every year. In my lease, the NNN can increase a maximum of 5% a year. So while our NNN costs are much higher than we are charging the tenants, we cannot increase those costs the entire amount. At the end of every year, we calculate our expenses, send a report to the tenants, and can increase the NNN if those expenses are more than they are currently paying (but not more than 5% each year).

Each lease will contain a different amount that the NNN costs can increase, and some may not have any restrictions.

How much does each tenant pay?

Something else that must be considered is what each tenant pays for NNN costs on a multiple-tenant building. On my big building, we have six tenants who share the property. How do we know how much each tenant pays? The way the leases were structured when we bought it was each tenant paid their share based on the percent of square feet they occupied.

- The grocery store occupies 82%, so they pay 82% of the NNN costs.
- The restaurant pays 10% because they occupy 10% of the building.
- And so on....

On top of the NNN costs and the base rent fees, the tenants pay their own utilities. Hopefully, the building has separate meters, or that can get tricky.

What would the total costs look like on an NNN lease?

Now that we know what is included on an NNN lease, or at least have an idea of what could be included on some, what do the total costs look like and how do we calculate them with rent?

The rent on a commercial building is often calculated using per-square-foot numbers. For example:

- The landlord is asking $10 a square foot and there are 5,000 square feet. The total rent would be $50,000 a year (10 x 5,000) or $4,166,67 a month.

On top of this cost, the tenant would be paying utilities, which could be from $100 to $1,000 a month based on the use, climate, and type of building.

Now we have to add the NNN cost, which may range from $1 to $20 a square foot based on the use and costs. It is typical to see a $3-a-square-foot NNN cost in my area, which would add $15,000 a year or $1,250 a month.

Your base lease rent of $4,166.67 could easily turn into $6,000 a month.

Do NNN leases favor the landlord or tenant?

As you can see, there is no clear-cut NNN lease. The costs involved can vary greatly. Some people may even say the common NNN lease is not even an NNN lease at all but an absolute lease.

Whether the lease favors the tenant or the landlord depends on many factors:

- Did the lease come with tenant improvements?
- Are the costs calculated accurately?
- Were both parties aware of how the costs are split?
- Is the lease written clearly?
- Was the tenant given a discount on market rent?
- What condition is the property in?

NNN leases can be great for both parties or horrible for either party based on these factors and many more. Some of my properties use NNN leases and some use gross leases. They both have advantages and disadvantages for both parties.

What other types of commercial leases are there?

NNN leases are common on commercial real estate, but they are not the only type of lease used. There are many types of leases, and they have slightly different definitions based on who you talk to, but here are the basics.

NN lease

This is very similar to the NNN lease, but only property insurance and property taxes are paid by the tenant. The maintenance is covered by the landlord, but the tenant still pays the utilities in most cases.

Net Lease

The tenant may pay a portion of the taxes based on their share of the building but not maintenance costs or insurance.

Absolute Lease

The tenant pays for everything and may even be responsible for taking care of everything. If the roof starts leaking, the tenant may have to call their roofer and get him over to fix it and pay him.

Modified gross lease

A modified gross lease is a mix of tenant- and landlord-paid expenses. The landlord typically pays the taxes and insurance, but the tenant still pays for their office expenses, such as janitorial. The utilities may be paid by the tenant or the landlord. The expenses can be split many ways, but with gross leases, the rent is usually higher than an NNN lease to make up for the extra expenses the landlord is paying.

Full-Service Lease or Gross Lease

The gross lease is when the landlord pays all the expenses including taxes, insurance, maintenance, utilities, and even janitorial service. The tenant just pays rent, which is usually much higher on a gross lease than an NNN lease.

Conclusion

There are many types of leases. We typically see NNN, absolute, and modified gross leases here. We rarely see NNN or gross leases, although they do exist. One thing is for sure—make sure you read the lease and know exactly what you are responsible for, whether you are the landlord or the tenant!

16

Repairs and Contractors

One of the most important and difficult parts of home ownership or investing in real estate is finding a great contractor. Contractors can be very expensive, take a long time to finish a job, or even quit on you. If you can find a good contractor with clear and detailed bids, great communication skills, and a great work ethic, it is awesome. I own 20 rental properties and complete 20-30 fix-and-flips a year, and contractors are vitally important to me. Buying a property is expensive, and repairing it can be even more expensive. If you don't have a great contractor, costs can skyrocket due to long timelines and increased repair costs.

What is the first step?

Finding a great contractor is not always easy and can take a lot of trial and error. My advice is to ask your friends, family, and co-workers for references before you try any other resource. When you get a recommendation, it does not guarantee that the contractor is good, but it gives you a place to start. Recommendations are usually a better sign of how good a contractor is than any advertising they do. A few people who may know a great contractor are real estate agents, property managers, or builders.

Anyone who owns a home may have used a great contractor at some point, so don't be afraid to ask your friends or family. You will still have to monitor that contractor to make sure they are doing what they promised. One of the easiest ways to let a rehab project get out of control is little or no oversight from the property owner when using a new contractor.

You must do more than trust a recommendation

I used a new contractor a few years ago. We are always trying out new people because of how many projects we have going. I got a recommendation from my broker and a couple of other agents in my office. The contractor was a builder and seemed to know what he was talking about and gave great, detailed bids. I put him to work on two property flips at once because I had a couple of properties waiting for work to be started. He told me he had a great crew and could handle as much work as I could give him. He ended up finishing one project on budget (always get a bid first), but the second project took two months to start!

I had assumed everything was going well since he told me it was, but the property was 40 minutes away, and I had not visited to ensure the work was started. This was completely my fault. I was in for a big surprise when I went to visit the property, which I thought was almost done, and no work had been started!

I called the contractor, and he gave me a story about too many jobs and his workers getting sick. He had been telling me everything was going great and the work was almost done. Either he had not been overseeing his workers properly or he had lied to me. That job was eventually finished about 4 months after it was started and three months after it was supposed to be done. I never used that contractor again, not because it took so long to finish the job, but because he lied to me about the work being done or had not visited the site for months.

What are some other ways to find contractors?

Box Stores

Another way to meet great contractors visiting large stores early in the morning and noticing who is buying large amounts of supplies. The people buying materials are probably contractors, and they may be looking for more work. You know they have at least one job going since they are buying materials. Some stores will also give you the names and numbers of contractors they know. You usually have to be a frequent customer at those stores since they are not supposed to give out names or numbers.

Craigslist

I have hired many contractors through Craigslist, but you have to be careful. Contractors can post there for free, so you can get a wide range of people to interview. We often find affordable contractors on Craigslist because it is free.

Angie's List

We have had some luck here as the contractors have to pay to be listed. You may find slightly higher quality contractors here than on Craigslist, but that does not mean they are all good.

Thumbtack

You may find some good ones here, but you may also find some very bad ones!

HomeAdvisor

You must weed through many people on this site to find the good ones.

Facebook

We have found contractors on Facebook's marketplace, where they advertise their services, or in real estate investor groups. Facebook is a great place to snoop around when you find a potential contractor to see what they are posting!

Can you use contractor locator services?

Home Depot offers contractor services no matter where you are in the country. Even though they may be more expensive than a local contractor, they offer standard work and stand behind their work. I'm also aware of a couple other companies that offer regional or nationwide contracting services. These companies may not work with an investor that has only one small job, but if you can offer them consistent work in one area, they may be a great choice.

In my experience, these companies source contractors just like you would but charge a fee to do so. Even if you find a contractor using a nationwide company, make sure you vet them as if you found them.

How do you oversee a job?

It is always best to keep an eye on your contractor's work and schedule, whether it is the first time you have used the contractor or the 20th. In my experience, the more communication and oversight you provide on your properties, the better job the contractor will do. I've worked with some contractors on over 20 jobs, and if I don't keep on them, they will get very slow. If a contractor does a great job once, it does not mean they will always do a great job.

I fired a contractor who had worked on many properties for me and had done a great job. He stopped visiting his worksites and started telling me jobs were done when they were not. His prices went up, and the time he took to finish jobs increased because he was never at the site and did not keep track of his workers.

Unfortunately, this happens quite a bit. Contractors get complacent or they try to push how much they can charge or how little work they can do and get away with. Contractors aren't the only ones who do this: it happens in every business. You cannot assume everything is being done as it should no matter how many jobs you have done with a contractor.

Here are a few tips on how to make sure your contractor is doing a great job.

- Constant communication
- Visit the property often
- Always get a written bid first
- Get a written estimate for when the work will be finished
- Don't prepay for any unfinished work (This is not always possible. Some contractors require a deposit upfront for material cost, but do not pay for the entire job.)
- Help pick out materials and paint colors

How do you interview a contractor?

We usually find contractors online. We go through a strict interview process before hiring anyone.

Get a resume

First, we always ask for a resume or a basic idea of what they can do. We ask this in the ad or in the first communication. Most contractors will not answer basic questions, and that eliminates many people (I make the checklist we use for contractors available to my coaching students).

Phone calls

If they answer our questions and seem decent, we call them before meeting in person. I want to make sure they know what they are talking about, and I want to get an idea of what they charge. A contractor should tell you their hourly rate, how many people are on the crew, and how long it takes to do an average job. I also want to know how busy they are and how many other customers they are working with.

Meet for lunch

If I like what I hear on the phone, I will set up a meeting at my office or restaurant. I will see if they show up on time, if they are driving themselves (to weed out those with DUIs), and how they seem to be in person. I don't want to work with someone I am not going to be able to get along with.

Get a bid

If that meeting goes well, I will schedule a time to meet them at a job site. I will go over what I want to be done and have them write up a bid for me. If you are new to real estate and finding contractors, always get multiple bids so you know you are not getting ripped off. Try to talk to the contractor as much as possible and learn about their family and what kind of jobs they normally do. In my experience, contractors like to talk a lot, and if you get them started talking, they may tell you some things that will help you make a decision. One contractor mentioned he had two recent DUIs, including one while he was on the job!

After I meet with the contractor, I will ask them to write up a bid and email it to me or call me when it is done. This is another test to see how quickly they get me a bid and if they get back to me. I've dealt with contractors who have never responded to a bid request. Eliminating them was easy.

I also like to start them on a small job first or part of a big job to see how they actually work. That way I am not on the hook for a massive project that they cannot finish.

How do contractors vary between investors and homeowners?

There is a huge variance in the amount of money different contractors charge. Some contractors will charge $40 an hour and others $100. $100-an-hour contractors may do amazing work, but most homeowners and investors will not need that expensive of a contractor. Most investors who are flipping or buying rentals will not be able to afford a contractor who charges that much. Many contractors do not like working with investors because they know investors won't pay as much as homeowners.

Many homeowners have no idea how much repairs should cost, so they hire a contractor and pay the cost. Most investors have a good idea of what the repairs should cost and are savvier when it comes to dealing with contractors. If you are remodeling your kitchen in a $200,000 property, it should not cost $50,000! It should cost less than $20,000 or even less than $10,000 depending on how fancy it is.

Why would contractors work with investors?

You may be asking why a contractor would work with investors when they can make more money working with homeowners. The reason is working with investors can be advantageous. When a contractor works with me, we can keep them busy full time. They do not have to spend any money or time on marketing. They do not have to buy materials because we pay for them. They do not have to worry about when they can work around the homeowner's schedule because they are working on vacant homes. Many contractors prefer working with us as opposed to always having to chase down the next customer.

Why do you need to monitor your contractor?

Contractors can get too busy, take too big of a job, or not keep track of their workers well. Any of these circumstances can cause a job to take too long or not be done correctly. Constant communication, written agreements, and monitoring a job are all keys to making sure your contractor does what they promised.

Always walk through a job site

If you have worked with a contractor on multiple jobs and know they know what you want, you may skip walking a job. I think it is always a good idea so they know what needs to be done. Make sure the contractor is writing things down when you are discussing what needs to be done. I've seen a few contractors write nothing down when I discussed exactly what I wanted to be done, and when I came back to the worksite, they were doing things I had not asked for and had not done things I did ask for. If the contractor doesn't write anything down and is trying to remember all the work that needs to be done, it's a bad sign.

Always get a written bid

You need to have a written bid when you have any work done on a property. A written bid serves multiple purposes that will save you time and money.

- A written bid makes sure both the contractor and the homeowner know exactly what services and repairs are being done. You don't want any confusion.
- A written bid lists the price that the contractor is charging for specific work. You don't want to be surprised with a massive bill for work you never agreed to. A written bid helps keep the contractor honest.
- A written bid may also include a timeframe for the work. Some investors will add incentives for getting a job done quickly. The faster they finish, the more the contractor gets paid.

Most contractors require bids be signed by both parties. The written bid not only keeps both parties honest, but the bid also reminds everyone of the scope of work. I have many jobs going at one time, and I tend to forget what was talked about. By having a written bid, there is no confusion about what was repaired and what it costs. Remember, a written bid does not guarantee everything will be alright. The only way to enforce that bid or contract is to sue the contractor.

Keep in constant contact

If you never hear from your contractor, that doesn't mean things are going great. I thought one job was going well because I never heard a thing from a contractor. I assumed he would have told me if there were any problems or delays. It turns out he had never started the job! Call your contractor to get updates on the job, and stop by the site to see how things are progressing.

Don't be afraid to ask your contractor if they are on schedule and budget. Ask your contractor if there are any changes to the bid or if there is any more work that needs to be done. If there are any changes to the work, make sure the contractor contacts you to approve the changes. Some contractors take it upon themselves to change a job or add work without asking the homeowner.

If the contractor is working on a property you don't occupy, you have to check on them. Some of my biggest failures with contractors happened because I was not visiting job sites. I think you have to visit the job site at least once a week to make sure work is being done. Do not tell the contractor you are coming, either. One contractor put 6 guys on a site when he knew I was coming. When I showed up to that job unannounced, no one was there!

Don't pay for unfinished work

Some contractors want partial payment before any work is started. If you have worked with a contractor before and this is their policy, it may work to pay them a portion to get started. You never want to pay more than 25 percent of the job up front. Before you pay anything, you need to vet them by checking reviews and references, if possible. One way to get around paying a contractor up front if they insist is offering to buy materials. We pay for all the materials on our jobs, and we mainly use Home Depot.

A contractor can place a lien on a home if they are not paid for completed work. Tracking down a contractor who takes their money before any work is done and skips town is much more difficult. The contractor has a much easier time collecting for unpaid work and should have no problem getting paid after a job is done.

Do a final walk through

A contractor should take pride in their work and be happy to show you what was repaired. I always do a final walk through to make sure the work was done correctly. Often, I must have the contractor go back and fix minor things or things we didn't notice the first time we looked at the home. Don't be afraid to point out work that you do not think is done correctly. If the contractor is hesitant about fixing it correctly, stand your ground. If the contractor refuses to make repairs or do things correctly, you know not to use them again.

Should you use subcontractors or general contractors

You have a couple of options when repairing rental properties, flips, or even your personal residence. You can use a general contractor who will do everything and hire all the work to be done. Or, you can hire subcontractors who will each do specific jobs. Hiring subcontractors takes more work from the homeowner but can save a lot of money. Using a general contractor can make the process easier but can also cost a lot more. I have used both options, but I like to use subcontractors for as many jobs as I can for multiple reasons.

How does using a general contractor work?

When you use a general contractor to do the entire job, they will handle almost everything that needs to be done. They will determine the entire scope of work. They will hire subs, create schedules, budget, and plan the entire project. Using general contractors can get very expensive because they do everything. The other problem with using general contractors is they can be very slow if they have to do all the repairs on a property. Some contractors may be able to handle huge jobs and get them done on time, but others may struggle.

How does using subcontractors work?

When you use subcontractors to, you have to hire out certain jobs and schedule the work. The benefit of hiring out specific jobs is they can be done more quickly and cheaply. Often, subcontractors will specialize in just one thing, like:

- Electrical.
- Plumbing.
- Roof.
- Foundation.
- Sewer.

- Landscaping.
- Flooring.
- HVAC.
- Drywall.
- Kitchen and baths.
- Paint.
- Windows.

Subcontractors can save money because that is the only job they do and they are really good and fast. A general contractor has to use their own crew or hire out a crew to complete jobs. While a general-contracting crew can usually do many jobs, they are not as fast or have the expertise of a sub who specializes in one thing. Many general contractors will also try to have most of the work done by their crew, which takes a lot of time.

Subcontractors can do multiple jobs at once, which saves a lot of time. The roof, plumbing, and electrical can be done simultaneously. Some of my biggest contracting problems came from giving an entire job to one contractor. They got overwhelmed and took forever, and one basically quit on me.

Please check state laws regarding repairs. Some states have stricter guidelines for who must be licensed and how to use subs.

How do we repair rentals and flips?

I have tried many ways to repair my flips and rentals. I have used general contractors, subs, hired an employee to run my projects, and even did the work on a flip myself. I have had some luck with general contractors, but they often bite off more than they can chew and over promise and under deliver. I think most contractors will say they can handle everything, and may even believe it, but are not equipped to handle large remodels on their own. I have had really good luck using subs for parts of jobs and then contractors for the majority of the work. Here is an example:

Subcontractor jobs:

- Electrical
- Plumbing
- Roof
- Landscaping
- HVAC

Contractor jobs:

- Replace doors
- Replace windows
- Paint
- Kitchen
- Baths
- Fixtures

While the contractor is working on their jobs, the subcontractors can be working on their jobs. In cases like this, I do not use a general contractor because I do not need someone to schedule and hire everyone. I would do the scheduling and hiring, or someone on my team would.

I hired a full-time employee to handle the hiring, scheduling, and project management on my rehabs. I thought this would be a great way to give myself more time and possibly start a new business in the future (contracting for other people). However, this venture has not gone as well as I hoped, and we are bringing the management back in-house for my team to handle. My new plan is to hire as many subs out as I can. Here are the benefits:

- I should be able to get jobs done faster because I will not have to wait on a contractor to have time to complete a big job. I will have a list of subs and can use the ones that are able to get work done the fastest.

· I will be able to save money because subs are usually cheaper due to the reasons we already discussed.

· I won't be relying on one contractor to get things right. If a subcontractor messes up, they will only mess up part of the rehab, and other work can still be done. If the contractor messes up, it can screw up the entire project.

I will still use some contractors and still look for great new contractors to repair my properties. Maybe someday I will find that magical contractor who is affordable, has a huge crew, is honest, and is fast. When I'm doing ten flips at once, finding contractors that can handle that much volume without falling behind is tough.

Is it smart to start using subcontractors right away?

The more experience you have, the easier finding subcontractors and hiring jobs out will be. If you have no contacts and must find all new subs from scratch, it can be a bit daunting. It might not hurt to try to find a general contractor and then slowly start looking for subs. If you are just starting out, try not to take on huge remodel projects that require an awesome contractor or many subs. As your business matures and you gain more experience, you will meet good subs and contractors. Make sure you keep track of their names and contact information!

Doing the work yourself versus using contractors

In 2006, in an effort to save money, I did all the work on a flip myself. It was one of the worst mistakes I ever made. I was miserable, it took me forever, and it ended up costing me money. Not only was I miserable, but I also lost so many opportunities because I spent all my time at that property. I learned never to do the work myself! For some people, it might make sense, but many people have a very unrealistic mindset towards what it actually takes to fix up a property.

Conclusion

Finding and watching over contractors is one of the most important parts of being a real estate investor. If you are a homeowner, doing a few things mentioned in this section can save you a ton of money. Do not assume your contractors are awesome and will always do what they are supposed to do. You have to spend time finding them, vetting them, and keeping tabs on them.

17

Be Prepared for the Waiting Game!

When I was looking to buy my first big commercial real estate deal, I used a commercial real estate agent because I knew just enough to get myself into trouble. I wanted help figuring out the steps to finding and buying a great commercial property. That agent did help me find a great property, and it has been the best deal of my life.

I am a residential real estate agent and have sold thousands of homes for other people and hundreds of my own properties. There is a major difference between commercial and residential agents. I think most commercial agents will admit this as well, but they tend to take things a little slower.

When I am making an offer on a residential property, I act fast. I want my offer to be submitted as soon as possible after I decide I want to try to buy the property. I can send an offer to the the real estate agent representing the seller an hour or two after a property is listed on the MLS. I often waive my inspection, and I am able to close in a couple weeks...or even sooner if needed.

When I made my first offers on commercial properties, I acted fast because I did not want to miss out on the deal. What happened? I got no response. I waited days, and I got very antsy. I thought they must be getting offers that were better than mine. Finally, I would call the other agent and see what was going on. They were sometimes annoyed that I was calling them so soon. They said they will get an answer, but it might take a little bit of time since the seller has to think it over. I was making these offers on properties that were $100,000 to $150,000. They were not million-dollar properties!

I ended up buying a few properties, waiting so long so long when I was used to acting so fast to get great deals was excruciating. I even submitted one offer that never received a response. I could not get the agent to email or call. It was a property that I was not too sad to lose, but I could not believe they simply never responded.

Over a month ago, I submitted an offer on a 20,000-square-foot property. I have still not received a response from the seller. The listing agent has talked to me numerous times and said he is trying to get the seller to respond, but they are pretty busy. This happens over and over with commercial real estate.

I recently hosted a commercial brokers meeting in my office, and several attended. One of them was complaining about doing a residential deal because everyone wanted everything to happen so fast!

I am not saying commercial real estate agents are bad or lazy, but commercial real estate is much different than residential. Deals can take years to put together, and agents are used to waiting and not feeling any pressure to get things done.

While waiting for responses and for deals to come together can be frustrating, waiting can be useful. I have completed a couple of 1031 exchanges, and because commercial deals can take so long, completing a 1031 exchange is much easier.

If you use a 1031 exchange to sell one property and then exchange the proceeds into a new property, you will defer all capital gains taxes...assuming everything is done properly. Most investors will sell their property and look for a new property to exchange into. You have 45 days to identify new properties and 180 days to complete the closing.

When I completed my 1031 exchanges, I found properties I wanted to buy, got them under contract, and then listed the properties I wanted to sell. Most sellers have no problem with a 90-day or longer closing on commercial rentals, which gives me enough time to list the property and get it sold before buying the new property.

The general timeline for these deals is usually longer. Instead of waiting 10 days for an inspection, you may wait 45 or 60. The bigger the deal, the more time you get to complete your due diligence.

This is why I was really glad that I used a commercial real estate agent to help me buy my first big deal. He knew what was customary what to ask for when we wrote our offer. He taught me many things about the entire process.

It does not hurt to try to act fast on commercial deals. I still act fast if I see a great deal because I do not want anyone else to beat me to it. However, be prepared to wait, and wait, and wait.

18

Taxes, Opportunity Zones, and 1031 Exchanges

Real estate can be a great investment thanks to cash flow, properties that can be bought below market value, leverage, and value adds. However, one of the best reasons to invest in real estate is the tax advantages. Commercial real estate offers some amazing tax advantages, but they are a little different than residential real estate. Like with residential properties, you can use a 1031 exchange to sell a commercial property and buy another while deferring the taxes owed.

Why does the government give preferential tax treatment to real estate?

The government wants people to buy properties because it is one of the best ways to help the economy. The more properties they can get people to buy, the better the economy usually does.

Rental properties commonly produce a profit, but thanks to depreciation, you can still show a loss on your taxes. You can also deduct the interest portion of a loan on a rental property or perform a 1031 exchange, which allows you to sell a property without paying capital gains taxes.

Please consult an accountant for specific tax questions

This information is meant to offer a broad overview of the tax advantages from rental properties, not specific advice. I am not an accountant or an attorney, and if you are looking for tax advice, please talk to a tax professional. Also, several online tax calculators and estimators can assist you. This section gets much of its information from the IRS tax code on rental properties.

Tax-deductible mortgage interest

The interest you pay on a rental property can be a deduction on your tax return. Your entire payment cannot be deducted because part of your payment is equity pay down, which is not deductible. Equity pay downs are not considered a business expense since the money is not spent on repairs or maintenance: it's used to reduce debt.

Depreciation

The IRS treats the rental property as a depreciable asset. They assume the rental property will slowly degrade over time until it is worthless. Most properties are not going to crumble into a pile of rubble unless they are not maintained, which is very good for rental property owners.

The IRS says a property will last 27.5 years, which means an investor can deduct the cost basis of the rental property in equal increments over 27.5 years. To calculate the amount that can be depreciated, divide the cost basis by 27.5. That is your deduction for the next 27.5 years. For example:

- A property sells for $150,000, but the structure is worth $120,000.
- The structure can be depreciated over 27.5 years.
- $4,364 can be deducted from your income, which can result in thousands of dollars in tax savings each year.

For commercial properties, the property is depreciated over 39 years. There was talk that the new tax law would reduce both residential and commercial depreciation to 25 years, but this clause did not make it into the final bill.

The cost basis is the cost of the rental property and only includes the structure of a rental property, not the land. If you buy a rental property for $100,000 that is on its own lot, the entire $100,000 is not the cost basis. You have to deduct the value of the land from the purchase price, and then you have a starting point for your cost basis. You can also add many of the closing costs—like abstract, title, recording, and other fees—to the cost basis.

Recaptured depreciation

If you depreciate a rental property over 20 years and sell the property, you could receive a large tax bill from the IRS. Rental property depreciation must be recaptured, which means you have to pay back all those taxes you saved with the depreciation deduction. The depreciation is only recaptured if you sell the asset for at least the amount of your cost basis minus the depreciation.

Even though you must pay back those tax savings, it is still better to pay those taxes 20 years down the road. With inflation, money is worth less in the future, and you can also invest that money for 20 years until you have to give it back to Uncle Sam. Think of it as a no-interest loan from our government! You also may be paying a lower tax rate on depreciation recapture than you would on ordinary income depending on your tax rate. The depreciation recapture rate is 25 percent, where ordinary income rates can be much higher. Additionally, there are many ways to avoid depreciation recapture.

Taxes on rentals when selling

- The easiest way to avoid paying back the tax savings is to keep the rental property and never sell it. You can refinance the property and take money out with a new loan without paying taxes.
- Another way to avoid the depreciation recapture is to use a 1031 exchange. If you sell your rental property, the IRS allows you to exchange that property for a similar property without having to recapture any depreciation.
- If you happen to pass away while you own your rental properties, the properties will pass on to your heirs. When your heirs inherit the properties, the cost basis becomes the current value of the properties, not what the original owners cost basis was. That means there will be no depreciation recapture. Planning to hold your rental properties until you die is not a bad strategy tax wise.

What other expenses can be deductible on rental properties?

Not every expense on rental properties is deductible, but many are. Since rental properties are considered a business, travel, accounting fees, management, and many other expenses can be deductible.

If you make repairs on your rental properties, they are deductible as well, but improvements are not. If you repair a leaky faucet, that is deductible, but if you add a second story, it is considered an improvement and not deductible.

Even though improvements are not deductible, you can use them to your advantage. Improvements can be depreciated. Improvement depreciation occurs over varying time frames, ranging from 3 to 20 years. You won't have to wait 27.5 or 39 years to see the full tax benefit from most improvements.

Maximum amount deductible on rentals

The IRS has different rules for those working in the real estate business. If you spend more than half your time on rental properties, you are considered to be in the rental property business, so there is no limit to the deduction or losses you can take on your rental properties.

If you are not in the rental property business, you can take a loss of up to $25,000 depending on how much money you make. The more money you make, the less of a loss you can count toward your other income. The deductions and depreciation will still counteract the money you make on the rental properties, but it might not help reduce your regular income taxes.

Rental Properties

Most real estate investors use LLCs or S corporations to do business if they do not simply pay taxes as an individual. When you operate these types of businesses, the income passes through the corporation to the individual. The recent tax bill includes a 20% deduction for pass-through entities. So, if you have a pass-through entity, you may pay 20% less taxes than you do now. However, there are some conditions:

- The service industry is excluded from this rule and would not get the deduction. From what I have heard, real estate agents, flippers, and landlords are not considered the service industry and will not have to worry about losing out on the deduction.
- You get the lower of the 20% deduction, 50% of your employees' w2's, or 25% of your employees' w2's and 2.5% of your investments (based on original purchase price). Basically, if you have multiple investments or employees, you will save a lot of money.

The new rules change the corporate tax rate from 35% to 21%.

- Landlords will still be able to deduct their interest from mortgages in full on rentals they own.
- Landlords will be able to deduct some expenses instead of depreciating them now.
- You can deduct more car expenses now (this is especially nice for agents).

The new tax brackets are much lower:

Taxable Income Level			Income Tax rates	
Married Filing Jointly	(Single Taxpayers)			
	Current	Proposed	Current	Proposed
Not Over:	$18,650 ($9,325)	$19,050 ($9,525)	10%	10%
Not Over:	$75,900 ($37,950)	$77,400 ($38,700)	15%	12%
Not Over:	$153,100 ($91,900)	$165,000 ($82,500)	25%	22%
Not Over:	$233,350 ($191,650)	$315,000 ($157,500)	28%	24%
Not Over:	$416,700 ($416,700)	$400,000 ($200,000)	33%	32%
Not Over:	$470,700 ($418,400)	$600,000 ($500,000)	35%	35%
Over:	$470,700 ($418,400)	$600,000 ($500,000)	39.6%	37%

Property taxes

When I was first buying rentals, property taxes on homes that cost $80,000 to $140,000 were around $400 to $800 a year. But, Texas may see property taxes 3 or 4 times higher than Colorado, and New Jersey has even higher taxes. When investing in real estate or buying a personal property, knowing what the property taxes are and how they affect you is important.

You may wonder why property taxes vary so much from state to state, but there is a simple explanation. Some states have no income tax; some have a high-income tax; some have no vehicle taxes; and some states have no sales tax. If you live in these states, the taxes are paid one way or another to the state. But when you are investing in rental properties from another state, you don't care what the income or vehicle taxes are.

One downside to commercial properties in Colorado is the property taxes are much higher than they are on residential. I might pay $1,000 a year for taxes on a $200,000 residential property, but I could pay as much as $4,000 a year on a $200,000 commercial property!

Tax advantages can be confusing. Always talk to an accountant or an attorney for specific advice. If you are looking to reduce your taxes, real estate can definitely help, but it can also make you a lot of money if you buy the right properties. The right corporate structure can also help greatly reduce taxes, so make sure you are not missing out by doing it all on your own.

1031 Exchange

A 1031 exchange allows you to sell a rental property and defer the taxes on any profit you make or on recaptured depreciation. A 1031 exchange has many rules and regulations, and you have to make sure you complete the exchange correctly to avoid a large tax bill from the IRS.

How does the exchange work?

A 1031 exchange allows an investor to sell one or more investments and buy new investments without paying taxes on the gain. Here are the basics:

- You can sell one property and replace it with one or more properties.
- The new properties must be worth at least as much as the property you sold (if you sold a property for $200,000, the new properties must be bought for at least $200,000).
- Any cash you receive from the sale of properties would have to be used to buy the new properties.
- An intermediary has to hold all the cash from the sales until it is used for the new purchases.
- You do not pay taxes on the recapture of deprecation, but your depreciation schedule does not start over. If you depreciate $50,000 off

the structure of a property, that $50,000 would carry over to the new property. If the value of the new structure was $100,000, you could only depreciate $50,000 of it.

How can you avoid taxes?

A 1031 exchange is a real estate transaction that involves two like proper-ties—one being sold and one being bought within a certain timeframe. There are many restrictions, and the IRS is not perfectly clear when describing the restrictions. Some basic principles are the properties must be held at least a year, be used for business, and the replacement property must be identified within 45 days and bought within 180 days. If all of these requirements are met, along with a few others, a rental property can be sold without paying any taxes on the profit or recaptured depreciation.

Which taxes do you owe in a normal sale?

When you sell a rental property, you have to pay taxes on any profit you make. You also may have to pay recaptured depreciation. The IRS allows you to depreciate a rental property because they feel the structure has a limited life span and decreases in value every year. You can deduct that depreciated amount from your taxes every year, which is a huge advantage to owning rental properties. However, if you sell the rental property for more than its depreciated value, you will have to pay back those taxes you saved.

Residential rental properties are usually subject to a 27.5-year depreciation schedule, and commercial rental properties are on a 39-year schedule. Each year you deprecate 1/27.5th of a residential rental, or .03636363636364%. You also only depreciate the structure of the property, so if you had a $100,000 property with a lot value of $10,000, you would calculate depreciation on the $90,000 value of the structure. Each year, you would depreciate $3,272.

When you complete a 1031 exchange, you can sell the depreciated property without paying taxes on the profit or depreciation. When you buy the new property, you still have the same depreciation schedule (it does not start over).

Here is an example:

- A property is bought for $100,000 and the structure is worth $90,000.
- Over ten years, more than $32,000 is depreciated from the property. That money can be deducted from your income on your taxes.
- If you sell the property for $100,000, the $32,000 would show as recaptured depreciation on your taxes, and you would pay taxes on it.
- You pay ordinary income tax on the depreciated income maxed out at 25% plus the 3.8% net investment income tax, if applicable, not at capital gains rates.

If you make a profit on the property, buy for $100,000, and sell for $200,000, you would pay taxes on the profit at the long-term capital gains rate. That rate is either 15% or 20% based on your income. If you don't use a 1031 exchange, you could end up paying $20,000 to $30,000 in taxes after selling the rental property:

- $32,000 times 25% = $8,000
- $100,000 times 20% = $20,000
- Total $28,000

How much does a 1031 exchange cost?

This can vary based on the company you use to complete the process, the type of exchange, and the number of properties involved. One company I used for my 1031 exchange charges:

- $700.00 at the first sale closing.

- $500.00 for each sale or purchase after the first one.
- $4,500.00 on top of the regular fees for title holding in a reverse exchange.

Another company I recently found charged me $500 for both the sale and purchase of a new property.

Do you have to depreciate a property?

Yes. This is an IRS requirement that makes you take the deductions.

Which properties are eligible?

The IRS has determined that many forms of real estate can be used for a 1031 exchange, including any property used for a business like stores, manufacturing facilities, or office buildings. Investment property can also be used in a 1031 exchange. This includes rental properties. It has even been determined that water rights and mineral rights qualify for a 1031 exchange. These cannot be used for a 1031 exchange:

- Stock in trade or other property held primarily for sale
- Stocks, bonds, or notes
- Other securities or evidences of indebtedness or interest
- Interests in a partnership (later, I will discuss a major exception to this one)
- Certificates of trust or beneficial interests
- A Chose in action (a right to something, such as payment of a debt or damages for injury, that can be recovered in a lawsuit)

Can property flips be used?

The IRS has determined fix and flips cannot be used for a 1031 exchange unless you meet certain guidelines. The IRS does not want real estate investors who constantly flip property to be able to use a 1031 exchange to defer taxes. If you only flip occasionally and meet these guidelines, you may be able to use a 1031 exchange:

1. The flip must be rented for at least one year after it is repaired.

2. The home cannot be sold until after it has been rented at least one year and should not be listed before being rented for a year.

The problem with this strategy is the IRS does not say you have to hold a flip one year to do an exchange. The IRS simply says a flip list shall be held for an acceptable amount of time, and it is up to the accountant and investor to determine if their transaction qualifies. Some people have determined that to be a year, but if the IRS thinks you are a professional property flipper trying to cheat them out of money, you still may get in trouble.

Others say you only need to own the property one year, without being rented, for it to qualify. Talk to professionals to figure out what strategy you want to use.

How do you complete the exchange?

When completing a 1031 exchange, the investor must use a qualified inter-mediary to oversee the transaction. The IRS does not tell you who can be an intermediary, only that these people cannot be:

- The taxpayer's attorney
- The taxpayer's CPA
- The taxpayer's real estate agent

- Any relative of the taxpayer's
- Any employee of the taxpayer's
- Any business associate of the taxpayer's

The intermediary holds the funds in the 1031 exchange after one property is sold and uses that money to buy the replacement property. The owner must identify the property they are exchanging and declare it before the sale. Once the subject property is sold, the investor has 45 days to identify a new property to exchange with the old property. Once the new property is identified, the investor has 180 days to close on the new property.

Can you identify multiple properties?

You have 45 days to identify a property or properties to exchange into. There are three rules for how you can identify the properties.

Identify three properties

The investor may identify up to three replacement properties and may acquire one, two, or all three of those.

Identify 200% of the sale price

The investor can identify more than three properties. The 200% rule says the taxpayer can identify any number of replacement properties as long as the total fair-market value of those identified is not greater than 200% of the fair-market value of the sold property. If you sold a property for $300,000, you could identify 6 properties worth $100,000 and still be within the rules since 200% of $300,000 is $600,000.

Buy 95% of the properties identified

The 95% rule says a taxpayer can identify more than three properties with a total value greater than 200% of the value of the relinquished property, but only if the taxpayer acquires at least 95% of the value of the properties identified.

How is the money handled?

To avoid paying taxes, the investor must use all the cash from the sale of the property to buy the new property. The new property must cost at least as much as the sale price of the old property to avoid paying taxes as well. If the investor does not use all the cash from the sale of the old property or buys a cheaper property, they may have to pay taxes on the unused cash or price difference in the properties.

The reason the investor has to buy a property that is just as expensive as the sold property is liabilities must be considered. If you sell a property for $200,000 that has a $100,000 loan and exchange it into a $100,000 property, you still realized a gain. You used all of the cash from the first sale to buy the second property, but you also paid off $100,000. That paid-off debt can be considered a gain.

How is the title taken?

The investor must take title to the new property in the same name as was on the property being replaced.

You also cannot use a 1031 exchange to sell a property to someone you are related to.

Can you use exchange money for repairs?

You cannot use exchange money to make repairs after a property has been purchased. It would be outside the exchange and could make the transaction taxable. If you plan to make repairs to a property you are buying in an exchange, the seller must make the repairs before closing and raise the price to account for the repairs. If that is not an option, you may have to use other non-exchange funds to make repairs.

What is a Reverse 1031 exchange?

Most investors will sell a property they own and then purchase a replacement property. It is possible to buy the replacement property and then sell the original property. This can be a difficult maneuver because the investor will not have the cash from the sale of the original property to buy the new property.

It may make sense for an investor who is building a replacement property to exchange into it. It may take more than 180 days to build and buy a property, and that is why an investor would do a reverse exchange. This is appropriate for large companies exchanging manufacturing facilities or other unique buildings that must be built to spec and are not available on the market.

How can you get your money back out?

One way to get the cash out of a rental property you exchange into is to refinance the replacement property. You may have $100,000 in cash proceeds from a rental property you are exchanging. That money can be used to buy a replacement property through a 1031 exchange, but that is a lot of money to have locked up. If you refinance the property after buying it, you can take out some of that cash without paying taxes on it. The government does not consider refinance proceeds to be profit.

Can you use a personal residence?

It used to be possible to complete a 1031 exchange into your own personal residence. The replacement property must be rented for at least a year after the exchange is completed. Once that year is up, you move into the replacement property and live there for at least two years. Since you are living in the home for at least 2 out of 5 years, your profit could be tax-free!

I have heard that the IRS has tried to limit this type of transaction, so talk to your accountant!

Why I did not complete a 1031 exchange on my rentals

I recently sold two of my rental properties. I was thinking about completing a 1031 exchange when I sold those rentals, but I kept the cash from the sales. There are a few reasons why I did this, and most of them had to do with not being rushed into buying a replacement property since I'd only have 45 days in a 1031 exchange to identify a replacement property or properties and would have had to buy properties that cost at least as much as what I sold the previous property for. Since I am not buying rental properties in Colorado at this time, I would have to find replacement properties in a new market with a new lender, with very little time to do it. I paid more taxes by not completing a 1031 exchange, but that doesn't mean I wasn't in as good of a financial position. By rushing to buy new properties, I may not purchase as good of a deal or may not learn a market as well as I would like to before investing.

How I Completed a 1031 exchange

While I sold my first rentals without doing a 1031 exchange, I recently completed a 1031 exchange with another rental. I was able to complete everything on time, but getting the timing right was tough. I already had a property I wanted to buy under contract, and I needed to sell a rental quickly. Here is how it went:

- I found a $600,000 commercial rental.
  I got it under contract with a 2-month closing time frame.
- I had a rental property that was vacant and was planning to sell.
- I listed it for sale after making some minor repairs.
- I was hoping to do a regular 1031 exchange, but my backup plan was to do a reverse exchange if we could not get the rental property sold in time.
- We got the rental property under contract to sell within the set time frames!
- However, the lender for the buyers had some issues, and they had to extend closing past the closing date for the property I wanted to buy.
- I offered to pay a little extra to extend the closing on the property I was buying in order to complete a regular exchange and not have to complete a reverse exchange.
- The seller agreed. We closed on the first property on a Monday and bought the new property on Tuesday!

In 1031 exchanges, you must adhere to many intricacies and details in the IRS tax code. There are more types of 1031 exchanges and many more situations that investors will run into. Talk to an accountant or attorney to make sure you are following all the guidelines.

Opportunity Zones

I want to be clear that I am not the expert on opportunity zones. I know a lot about real estate, but I do not know everything. If you are really interested in opportunity zones, I suggest you find an expert on them, but in the meantime, I can give you some basic ideas about how they work.

The government has created opportunity zones to encourage people to invest in areas of the country that would otherwise see have much investment. This is directly from the IRS website:

"Qualified Opportunity Zones were created by the 2017 Tax Cuts and Jobs Act.

These zones are designed to spur economic development and job creation in distressed communities throughout the country and U.S. possessions by providing tax benefits to investors who invest eligible capital into these communities. Taxpayers may defer tax on eligible capital gains by making an appropriate investment in a Qualified Opportunity Fund and meeting other requirements."

Only certain areas are considered opportunity zones, and you should be able to find a map of the zones online. There are opportunity zones in my area, and I own a property in an opportunity zone. I am not sure how the opportunity zones were created, but in a state with a booming economy like Colorado, I was surprised to see so many areas deemed opportunity zones. There are even opportunity zones in Boulder, where median property prices are more than $1,000,000.

With my opportunity-zone property, I haven't done anything to take advantage of that designation. In order to take advantage of the opportunity zone, you must start a fund, invest at least as much money into the property or business as you bought it for, and hold it for at least 5 years.

If you hold the property long enough, you can defer taxes on previous capital gains and eliminate some of those taxes. You can also defer and eliminate some of the taxes you would incur by selling the opportunity zone property.

Conclusion

Taxes can be complicated, which is why I always have an accountant figure everything out for me. I highly suggest other investors do the same thing as it saves time and money for most people.

19

Working with Partners and Syndication

Getting into flipping or buying rental properties can be very difficult for aspiring investors. The biggest problem for most investors is finding the money to flip or the down payment for rentals. In some cases, an investor has a lot of money, but no time to find deals, renovate properties, or perform the other tasks needed to invest in real estate. In other cases, an investor may have the knowledge and time to invest, but no money. A partnership can be a mutually beneficial way to invest in real estate if done right.

I rarely partner with anyone in my business, but I used to partner with my father, and I have one partner on one property now. It would have been really tough for me to flip properties or sell real estate without a partner to help with the financing and mentoring. But, in some ways I think having a partner also held me back and provided a comfort zone that allowed to me to relax more than I should have. Having a partner can be a great way to get started, but if you don't set things up correctly, it can be a disaster and destroy relationships.

How does a partnership work?

Rental property partnerships can be even trickier than fix-and-flip partnerships. The tough part is knowing how the partnership will progress through time. One partner may want to cash out in five years and another partner may want to hold the properties for thirty years.

Calculating returns can also be a little tougher. When flipping, you know what the profit is after the sale. With rentals, you have equity pay down, tax advantages, appreciation, and cash flow. Some of these returns are in the form of cash in your pocket, like cash flow. Other returns, like appreciation and equity pay down, are not realized unless the home is sold or refinanced. Not only do you have to come up with a percentage of the actual profits (cash flow) that will be split, but you have to come up with a percentage of the equity that will be split if the properties are sold or if one partner wants to sell out and the other wants to keep the properties.

Here are some things to considers:

- **Who does the work**: Will both partners work to find properties, or will one do all the work? How will repairs and maintenance be handled? Who will screen tenants, or will a property manager do it?
- **How much money will each partner put in**: Will one partner put in all the money and the other do all the work? Will it be a mix of money and work?
- **What percentage of the profits will each partner take**: Calculating rental profits can be tough. You will have up or down cash flow months, and properties can be depreciated. With depreciation, tax returns will show less profit than you actually make. You also need to have reserves in place for maintenance and vacancies. You have to decide what each partners' role is worth and how profits will be split.
- **What percentage of equity does each partner get**: When you get a mortgage, the equity will slowly increase as payments are made, and

properties might appreciate. If you bought the property below market value, you also increase equity. That equity does no good unless you sell or refinance, but you need to figure out what percentage each partner gets if you sell or refinance.

- **What happens if one partner wants out**: The biggest problem with partnerships is ending the relationship. How long do you plan to own the property together? What if one partner needs money and wants out? What if the property doesn't make as much money as you thought and a partner wants out? You have to figure out, before the partnership starts, what will happen if one partner wants out how to end the relationship.

As you can see, things can get tricky. Determining the amount of work each person is responsible, the exit strategy, and the percentages each investor gets (and when), is tough.

Why does everything need to be in writing?

If you decide to enter a partnership, everything has to be in writing. I don't care if your partnership is with your brother and best friend, it should be in writing. There are multiple reasons why:

- **People forget things**: You'd think you would never forget the details of a partnership that involves thousands of dollars, but it happens. I wrote an article about private money and mentioned I pay my sister six percent interest. She read it and was quick to remind me I pay her seven percent! We put everything in writing so there are no mistakes or fall outs from simply forgetting the terms.
- **Partners need to know roles**: If you are doing a flip with a partner and decide to share the work, how much time will each person put in? One partner may have a family emergency or may have to work overtime. How many hours will each person put in, and what are the consequences if they don't pull their weight? One of the biggest problems is one partner thinks they do all the work while the other collects the profit without

doing anything.

- **Exit strategies**: You have to know what happens if one partner wants bought out or has to sell. How is market value determined? How will costs be split? Etc.
- **Use of professional services**: If one partner is a contractor or real estate agent, how will they be paid for their services? Will they get a higher percentage of the profits for their expertise or for saving money on commissions? Will the contractor or agent be paid like they would any other job?
- **Rates, terms payoffs**: If you are borrowing money from a partner, all the terms of the loan or agreement need to be in writing. Some agreements involve a pure profit split, but others might involve private-money lending with interest rates, length of the note, etc.
- **Decision making:** Who has the final say on how much money to spend, how to repair a property, what properties to buy, etc.? What happens if the partners don't agree? This is another big issue that can cause problems if they're not in writing.

A huge issue with partnerships arises when one side either forgets or does not live up to their agreed-upon obligations. If the obligations and consequences of not fulfilling them are in writing, the partnership will be much more successful. The partners will have more motivation to work hard, and handling problems when they come up will be easier.

Do you need a partner?

Many people ask me how to structure a partnership. One question I received was, "We have the money and knowledge to buy rentals, but we have the opportunity to partner with another investor. How do we structure it?"

My answer was, "Why do you need a partner?" Why bring someone in to share the profits on a deal when you have the money and know how? You will make much more money on real estate deals when you do not have a partner.

The purpose of a partner is to provide something that you cannot or do not want to provide. You give up some of the profits to spend less of your own money and use someone's time or their expertise. If you don't need any of those things, don't give up your profits!

Do you have anything to offer a partner?

I've learned many people are looking for a partner or a mentor to help them start investing. The problem is they want someone to show them how to buy properties, fix them up, find great deals, and make a ton of money. But, the person looking to be taught how to invest is offering nothing to the investor, except for a willingness to work hard.

I've received this proposal myself multiple times, almost every time, there are huge problems on my side of the deal.

1. When I ask them what they can offer me in return, they say determination, hard work, etc., but they list no specific skills. What can you do better than other people who will help me become more successful or help the deal be more successful? Are you good with computers? Do you have carpentry skills? Are you an expert marketer? Willingness to learn and hard work is not a skill, but everyone says they have those traits. If you want to impress someone, be as specific as possible about how you will help them make more money.

2. Most successful investors do not have time to train someone about the entire investing process. They also may not want to train someone who will eventually compete with them! Don't be put off if an investor does not want to mentor someone since it is a very involved, long process. Paying for knowledge and experience is also an option and shows you are serious. Most people who want free help and have nothing to offer in return won't even use that help if they get it, and it is a giant waste of time for everyone.

3. Many aspiring investors want someone to tell them how to do everything. People have come to me asking how to make money investing in reals estate. Well, I could write a book on that and still not answer all of their questions (actually, I did write a book on flipping). I point out articles or point them towards my book, and they don't want to take the time to read the articles or pay $12 for a book. They want everything done for them without doing any work. If you want to impress a potential partner or mentor, do your research and learn as much as you possibly can. The more knowledge you have, the better chance you have of impressing someone enough to help you.

If you want to be a partner in a real estate deal, you must have something to offer. You need to bring money, expertise, skills, or pay for the opportunity. There are no shortcuts to becoming a successful real estate investor.

Why did I end my real estate partnership with my father?

I partnered with my father and our real estate team before taking over everything in 2013. The partnership was great to help me get started after I graduated college in 2001. I could have never flipped properties out of college because I had no money and no way to finance all of the deal. In return for money to flip and knowledge, I gave up most of the profits. For a while, I was even doing the painting, and on one property, most of the repair work. When I did the work myself, I did not get a higher percentage—I was paid hourly. Flipping with a partner was great in the beginning, but at the end, I was doing almost all of the work, and I did not have the final decision on what to buy.

On our real estate team, my father paid the staff, took care of most expenses, and took a big chunk of my commissions. Not having to worry about payroll and everything else was nice, but I also sold most of the properties on the team, and I was giving up a lot of profit by having a partner. My father was also tired of running the team and managing all the people.

I had wanted to take over everything for a while, but was worried about the time it would take to manage it all and what my father would think. I approached him about it, and my parents said they were waiting for me to take over because they were ready to retire! My good friend was joining the team, and he could help with the transition. I also had a good relationship with my portfolio lender so I could finance the flips. I ended up buying out my parents and taking over the entire business. I love having complete control and keeping the profits!

Why partner on commercial deals?

Commercial real estate is a little trickier than residential real estate. When starting out, getting financing and identifying good deals is tougher. A partner in commercial real estate may make more sense because they can help in a number of ways.

-They can help you get financing if they have commercial investing experience.

-They can help you get your foot in the door to talk to to sellers.

-They can provide money since commercial deals are often more expensive.

-They can provide guidance and help new commercial investors avoid mistakes that may not be as noticeable with other niches.

Syndicating commercial real estate

I will be completely and totally honest with you—I am not an syndicator. I have never done a syndication deal, and I am the wrong person to talk to about syndication. I know how syndication works, but if you want to do these types of deals yourself, find an investor who does them.

A syndication deal is like a fund or even a stock. There is one person/entity/-group who finds the deal, manages it, and makes all the decisions. Another group of investors supply much of the money for the deal, but they do not have any decision-making powers.

Warren Buffet made millions using this model with stocks. A group of investors gave him $100,000, and Buffet used a few hundred dollars of his own money to start a fund. He made all the decisions for the fund and kept some of the profit the entire fund made. The other investors had no say in what Buffet invested in. They simply gave him money and hoped he would make them more money (which he did).

Real estate syndicators will often use their own money to buy large apartment or commercial complexes, but they will mostly use other investors' money. The investors will get paid a percentage on their money, maybe 8%, and the investors also may get a share of the profits when the building is sold or refinanced.

Getting financing on properties that are underperforming can be tough. If you can get enough money from other investors, you may be able to buy big projects without using banks. Then, when you get the property performing well, you can refinance or sell the property, cash out the silent investors, and keep the deal for yourself or take the majority of the profits in the deal.

This plan has made many people a lot of money, but as with anything, it is great in theory but harder to pull off in real life.

Some of the difficulties with syndication are:
Lining up the investors who will be willing to wait for you to find a deal.
Finding big deals that will work for syndication
Setting up the fund and making sure you abide by all the rules
Investing enough money yourself to handle earnest money and other costs

I have seen many investors who want to be syndicators never buy a deal, or it takes them years to find a deal and get it completed. It is not impossible, but realize it takes a lot of work and effort.

Conclusion

Partnerships can be a great way to get started if you need help. Partnerships can also be a nightmare if roles aren't clearly defined or nothing is in writing. Partnerships also evolve, and you may have to be flexible as people's priorities in life change. My partnership with my father changed over the years until I ended up buying him out. Everything was in writing, and that helped things go smoothly.

If you enter a partnership, make sure you take the time to set it up right. If you don't need a partner, having complete control and earning all the profits sure is nice.

III

Case Studies

The details on my proprieties.

20

Case Study #1: My First Commercial Property

I have purchased 10 commercial rental properties in the last few years, and I am going tell you all about each one! I got a great deal on all of them, and I bought them a number of different ways. I had different uses for each of them, and I plan to buy many more. If I think about it, I might even update this book as I buy more, or you can see all my rentals at https://investfourmore.com/rentals.

Rental Property Number 17

This was the first commercial property I bought, but it was not the first I got under contract. I have mentioned the first property that got me interested in commercial real estate, and that was rental number 20. The title issues on that property took a very long time to sort out!

I purchased number 17 from a friend of mine. We are not best friends but get along great the couple of times we see each other every year. I showed them my properties in the past, and they called me one day asking if I knew anything about commercial real estate. I thought that was ironic since I had just been getting into commercial properties!

It turned out he wanted me to help him sell a small commercial shop he had owned for a few years. He had bought it for his own use but did not need it anymore and was renting it to an import-car performance company. They wanted to leave, and he wanted to sell the building.

I mentioned I could help him sell the property or may be interested in buying it myself. I told him I wanted good deals and he might make more money listing it for sale, but I would not charge him a commission if I bought it. He thought about it and told me to make him an offer. I can't remember exactly how the negotiations went, but we settled on $72,500.

He was happy with that price, as was I. Although, to be honest, I did not know enough about commercial properties to be sure I got a good deal! I had a hunch it was decent, and I could use the shop immediately, which was the real reason I bought it.

Before I bought this shop, we had a couple of storage units for my property flipping business. We needed a place to put extra supplies for when Home Depot had clearance items or we had extra stuff. Those storage units were costing us a few hundred dollars a month. If I had my own shop, I would not need those storage units, and I would have a better place to store a car or two!

I am a car nut, and one of my cars is a 1991 Mustang 5.0 convertible. I added a supercharger and a few other goodies right after college, and that car was my daily driver for many years. I did not have room for the Mustang, so it was stored in one of my sister's garages. She owned a few college rentals that came with detached garages. Now, I could put the car in my own garage closer to my house.

The shop has been great the last three years and provided a lot of use for extra supplies, car storage, and hoarding. The hoarding is not really an advantage but has happened on occasion!

I bought the property with 25% down and used a local bank to finance it. I think my payment is roughly $400 a month! If I wanted to rent out the space, I think I could get $1,000 a month for it as there is high demand for this type of shop.

If I were to get that much money in rent, it would make the property worth more than $150,000! When I first bought the property, I did not know enough about CAP rates or rents to to think it would be worth close to that much. I looked at a few other places that were for sale in the same complex and based my price off them. This property is located in a complex with many shops just like it.

I am constantly evolving and changing. I may have an idea to move the flipping supplies to another place soon. That would free up this space to rent out, and we can see if I can get that $1,000 a month or not!

21

Case Study #2: 7,000-Square-Foot Office Building

Rental Property Number 18

This was a risky buy, and if it weren't for a mistake from one of my team members, I may not have purchased it.

I saw the property for sale on the MLS. I think there was a large price change that caught my eye. Again, I saw it was commercial and hesitated, even after opening up the MLS sheet (now, I love seeing commercial on the MLS). It was listed for $325,000 after being listed for $379,000 and $478,000 before the price changes. It was under contract a couple of times as well.

It was originally built to be a doctors office and was zoned for mixed use. The doctor had planned to run his business on the main floor and live in the basement. He had dug out a large portion underneath for an exterior exit in the basement, and it was a very neat property.

It was vacant, and the owner had wanted it vacant for some reason to sell it.

The most recent tenant was a veterinarian, and the owner had told them to find somewhere new. The owner thought that having it vacant would make it worth more because of its mixed use zoning. Someone could turn it into apartments, perhaps. They marketed it hard because of that mixed use, but they were having a hard time selling it.

I saw the property with my project manager Nikki, who helps me with everything. She does most of the work on the property flipping side of the business and helps with commercial rentals as well. She really liked the property and thought it had a ton of potential. However, it was vacant, and I did not know exactly how easy it would be to rent or exactly what it would rent for. I did not even know how much work we should or should not do to the place since it was a little bit outdated.

On top of all of this, the property was located in a small town of about 5,000 people. The town was very close to larger towns, but that made me nervous. After much discussion, we decided it would be a good deal and I should make an offer.

I asked her what she thought I should offer, and she said something like $315,000. I decided to offer $292,000 with $3,000 in earnest money. The listing agent said they loved my offer but wanted more earnest money, $10,000 to be exact. I agreed because I had a loan contingency and inspection period. They took my $292,000, which Nikki could not believe. I knew they had it on the market a long time and may take a low offer.

We went through some inspections for the HVAC, plumbing, and other major systems. The property was not in horrible shape, but it needed some work! I knew we would have to spend some money on it to get it up and running.

I was thinking of using a partner on this deal, but I had not worked that out before making an offer. I often like to get a property under contract first to get things locked down and then talk to potential partners. Maybe I am paranoid.

I talked to someone who I thought would be excited about it, and they did not like the deal at all. They were worried about the location, finding a tenant, and a number of other things. That worried me too because I thought they would be all in.

I then talked to a bank who I thought would love the deal, and they balked! Since the property was vacant, they did not want to lend on it and were worried about the other issues too.

I decided the best thing to do would be to cancel and get my earnest money back. Then, it happened.

I had asked one of my team members to write in an inspection- and loan-conditions period. Those contingencies allow me to get my earnest money back if I run into any problems, and I can terminate the contract within the dates for those contingents.

When I write offers on property flips, I almost never use contingencies. One of the ways I get great deals is by requiring no inspection or loan conditions. Well, that team member wrote the contract with no inspection or loan contingency. To be fair, I signed that contract without looking at it closely. I should have reviewed it closer, especially after the listing agent said they wanted $10,000 in earnest money.

Now I knew why they liked my offer!

I had a decision to make—buy the property and somehow come up with the $292,000 (well, technically $282,000) or terminate and lose my $10,000. I was ready to terminate and lose my $10,000 when Nikki convinced me to do everything I could to buy it. She was adamant about it being a great property and deal. I thought about it and decided it was worth a shot.

I could have come up with that cash, but it would have drained me. I do a lot of real estate deals, and often, my cash is tied up in many properties, not sitting in my bank accounts! I had developed a private-money relationship with the investor who I tried to partner with on this property.

By private money I mean he would lend me money to buy property flips. He makes 10% for doing nothing but lending money, and I can put less of my own money into the deals, which allows me to do more deals and make more money.

I asked him if he wanted to be the lender on this deal since he did not want to be a partner. He agreed! So I had figured out my money problem, and I would soon have a commercial property—a big commercial property—and my most expensive rental property by far. I think the most I had previously spent on a rental property was $140,000.

I bought the property, and we got to work trying to figure out what to repair and what not to repair. As a reminder, all of my rentals are on YouTube. If you want to see this property, search for "rental property number 18 and InvestFourMore."

The previous buyers had all thought about making this a residential property with apartments but had backed out because of the cost involved in converting everything to residential. The property was set up as an office with many small offices. It would take a lot of work to convert it to residential apartments. I think most of the buyers had assumed it needed to be residential because that was what it was being marketed as.

I decided the best use for the property was to keep it as commercial. It was set up for offices. It was in a decent location for commercial. Not converting it would save me a ton of money.

Repairing commercial rental properties is tricky because different tenants have different uses and will want the properties set up differently. You do not want to make a property specific to one type of business because another business may want the space and require something completely different. On the other hand, you want the space to look decent so that you do not scare away the tenants who may or may not think you are a slum lord.

We decided to do a basic remodel on this property, which turned out to be much more expensive than we thought it would be. We would paint, replace the flooring, add a small kitchen, add some granite counters, and replace fixtures. We would do all of this in the front unit.

Yes, this property had multiple units. It was set up as a two-unit property on the main floor. It had a basement with concrete and storage in one half and dirt floors in the other.

Then, something amazing happened. As we were remodeling the property, an agent happened to drive by, see we were working on it, and called me. He asked if it was going to be for rent, and he had the perfect tenant for it.

We met the agent and his client, who happened to run an oil field company. We had painted and added some flooring, and they loved it. They wanted the entire main floor, which was about 3,600 square feet, and the agent asked what we wanted for rent. I was not even sure what to say!

I looked back at the original marketing materials to see what the listing agent said about the rent. It said it should rent it out for $4,500 a month. I thought that was high considering the square footage, but then I noticed that was a gross lease, meaning the landlord paid for utilities, maintenance, etc.

I asked the agent what kind of lease they preferred, and they said they wanted a gross lease if possible. I proposed $4,500 for a gross lease, and they agreed! They asked for a few things to be customized in the space...but nothing crazy. I had rented out the space without even trying. I could not believe it.

I told the private-money lender that it rented for $4,500, and he could not believe it either. He said he sure wished he had been a partner with me on the deal instead of just the lender!

We finished the space, and the oil company moved in. We spent something like $80,000 on that remodel, which was way more than I thought we would. The big expenses were the electrical and the HVAC. All the heating vents were a weird paper substance with holes, and we had to replace it all. I made the mistake of using a commercial electrician because they charge commercial rates!

After getting the property rented, I approached a bank to get it refinanced. At this point, I had purchased a larger commercial property with that same private-money lender as the partner. His personal bank financed that property and said they could refinance this one for me as well.

We ordered an appraisal, and it came back at $450,000! I was thinking the property would be worth right around $450,000 or more with the gross lease we had in place, and it was nice to see my calculations justified by an appraiser. Of course, we had to spend like $2,500 on that appraisal.

I talked to the lender, ready to get similar terms as we had on the other deal. We did, and he threw a massive wrench at me. He said because we only had a three-year lease in place, they would only be able to offer a three-year term, which meant that after three years, they could call the loan due. That was a dealbreaker for me! They told me they would offer a ten-year term when I first asked for the loan.

I was pissed, but I did not give up. I talked to another lender, who was a friend of my brother in law and worked at another local bank. He looked at the numbers, saw the appraisal, and did the refinance with a ten-year term!

I did not get all of money back, but I was happy with the deal:

- I bought it for $292,000 with 100% private financing
- I spent $80,000 on the repairs
- I refinanced at 75% loan to value, which was about $337,000, giving me $40,000 and change cash back
- My payment is $1,900 a month, and we pay all utilities and maintenance.
- Very conservatively speaking, we make $1,500 a month from a $40,000 investment with $113,000 in equity
- As a bonus, we have 3,600 square feet of unfinished basement for storage or possible finish out in the future.

This was a scary property that I did not want to buy, but it turned out to be a great investment. The oil company could leave, but we did not do any crazy renovations for them that are super unique to their needs. If they do leave, it is a nice office that should appeal to many renters. It is still set up to have many small offices, like a vet, dentist, or doctor would have. We can also split it into two units on the main floor, which may make it easier to rent out.

In the future, we could finish the basement, which would add even more value. If we converted to residential, it would make the property more diverse and less affected by down markets. People will always need a place to live, but they will not always need a place to rent for their business.

Just for fun, I want to explore what would happen if we did finish the basement. Half of the basement is set up for medical storage, and we could probably rent that out if it had a decent outside entrance, but it does not at the moment. You can only access it through the middle of the upstairs office or the unfinished portion of the basement.

If we were to finish the dirt-floor side of the, we would gain about 1,800 square feet of living space. The basement unit is a dugout with tons of light, and the south wall has many windows that are partially above ground. It is not a dark, depressing basement but rather a somewhat light, large space.

The trick with the basement would be positioning the bedrooms because every one would need an escape or egress window. The south wall has those already, or we could add them on to the west wall. It would be feasible to create a 3-bedroom, 2-bath apartment with plenty of space and decent light. The weird thing is it's below a business, and when you walk outside, an A&W restaurant is literally staring right at you.

The real unknown about finishing the basement is what the actual cost will be. Finished-basement costs can be simple to estimate if you only need a bedroom, a family room, and maybe a bath. We are looking at an entire apartment with dirt floors, not plumbing, and major electrical work needed.

Here is my rough estimate of what it would take on the fly:

- Plumbing for a kitchen and two baths: $8,000
- Wiring for the entire apartment: $7,500
- Concrete: $12,000
- Bath finish: $4,000
- Kitchen Finish: $8,000
- Flooring: $5,500
- Drywall: $10,000
- Doors: $4,000
- Windows: $5,000
- Trim: $3,000
- Framing: $6,000
- Fixtures: $2,500
- HVAC: $5,000
- Miscellaneous: $10,000
- **Total: $95,500**

That is a lot of money to create an 1,800-square-foot basement apartment! I would not be surprised if the cost crept up to $100,000. Depending on what market you are in, that might seem crazy, or it might seem like a steal.

What would that basement finish bring us as far as rent and value add?

Time to do some more analyzing!

The first thing we must do is figure out what the rent will be after we finish the basement apartment. For an 1,800-square-foot apartment in this area, I would think the rent would be $1,600 to $1,800 based on the condition, location, and amenities. Though it's a basement apartment below a commercial business, it will be brand new with modern designs and features. This property is also in a somewhat small town that might have limited demand for rentals, or it might have massive demand that is not being met. That's the danger of small towns!

To be safe, we will estimate that the rent will only be $1,500 a month. However, it could easily be more.

That means we will be adding $18,000 a year in gross income. The resultant net income will depend on how the utilities are charged and if the landlord is paying any costs. The utilities do not have separate meters, which means the landlord will likely be paying them, or they will be estimated. If the utilities are included in the rent, we could charge more than $1,500 a month. The bills might be:

- $100 a month for electric.
- $100 a month for gas.
- $50 a month for water.
- $25 a month for trash.

That is almost $300 a month in savings for the tenant if we include all the utilities in the rent. The upstairs tenants have that same gross lease where the utilities are all included, so it might make sense to lease the basement the same way. If you are wondering, I am coming up with all of these ideas as I write the book. Not only am I hoping to teach you something, but I am teaching myself!

I think we should settle on $1,700 a month in rent with all utilities included. What does this look like as far as value add?

Since I already own the property and pay the property taxes and insurance, I do not have to figure those costs into the equation. I might have some more management costs and more maintenance costs with the new tenants:

- Management: $150 a month
- Maintenance: $150 a month
- Vacancies: $85 a month

My net income is $1,315 a month or $15,780 a year. What if we plug that number into my trusty CAP-rate calculator? At a 7 CAP rate, the property is worth $225,429 more than it was with the unfinished basement. At a 6 CAP, it's $263,000 more. That turned my $450,000 property into a $675,000 property.

$100,000 on a basement finish seems like a lot of money, but when you realize that it earns you $15,000 a year more and increases the value by more than $200,000, it may not seem quite as crazy.

I have to hand it to Nikki for convincing me to buy this property. It has been a great rental with great tenants, yet I was trying to figure out how to get out of the contract!

22

Case Study #3: A Steal From Facebook

Rental Property #19

This was an interesting buy. I flip a lot of properties, and if you follow me on Instagram, Facebook, or YouTube, you know that. I tell my contractors that if they ever find me deals, I will find a way to make it worth their while. This is the only deal my contractors have found!

One of my contractors said they saw a deal on Facebook Marketplace in 2017 when Facebook Marketplace was just starting. I am always skeptical when I hear someone say they found me a deal because my idea of a deal is not usually the same as other's idea of a deal. However, once in a while, they mesh, and things work out fantastically.

I looked up this property, and it was listed for $79,000 or $72,000 or something stupid cheap. Okay, I have to admit my contractor did me right on this one because it was a smoking deal. I was still in the infant stages of my commercial real estate ventures, but I knew this price was way too cheap.

The property was a small industrial shop with about 1,600 square feet and a quarter-acre lot. The property was one the outskirts of my town of about 100,000 people. I had seen the building growing up and vaguely recognized it.

I messaged the seller and told him I was interested in seeing the property. He mentioned he lived in Nebraska but would be in town in a few days and could show it to me. We met at the property. It looked a little beat up, but nothing crazy, and I thought *I need to have this*! I asked him how to make an offer, and the news hit.

He told me he had about 7 interested parties and was letting everyone make an offer through sealed bids.

My heart dropped a little because I was hoping I could buy it right then for $79,000 (or whatever he was asking). Now I knew I had some more work in store. I had to figure out what I could pay for the place while still making financial sense.

Based on my other commercial experiences, I thought it would rent for $1,500 a month or more. In the past, I would be happy to pay $130,000 or $150,000 for a residential rental that needed minimal work and would rent for that price.

I was still fairly new in the commercial real estate game. I kept asking myself why the price was so low. Does he know something I don't know? He seemed like a smart guy and had other real estate investments closer to where he lived. Somehow, I had to figure out what I should pay for this property. I wanted to get it, but I didn't want to pay $50,000 more than I had to.

When I am in a situation like this, I try not to get greedy. Many people will be really worried about what the other people will pay, but I simply had no idea what they will pay. I have to focus on what will make the deal work for me. I also have to try to ignore the cheap asking. Often, a very cheap asking price will make us send an offer that's too low, and we will get beat out.

I looked at the numbers, and I knew it was a good deal at way more than $80,000. There were a lot of unknown. I thought it was worth at least $150,000 as it was. I didn't want to pay $150,000 because I still want to get a good deal. How good of a deal do I need to make it work? Since these are commercial deals and I was still very knew to the game, I needed a really good deal.

I decided to offer $101,250. That is a weird offer! I like to make weird offers like that because I think round numbers are to easy to come up with. Many people may have thought this is a good deal. I think $100,000 is a fair offer.

I don't want to get beat out by someone who makes a round offer like that, so I usually go a little higher than the obvious offers of $100,000, $120,000, $175,000, etc. I also like to add a weird amount to the number I offer. I offer $101,000 because I want to beat out the $100,000 offers. I added the $250 because I want the seller to think I really thought about it.

If I make offers that have $250, $175, or even $167 in them, it looks like I ran those numbers hard and ended up on the exact amount I could pay, which makes it look like I went deep to come up with an exact amount. That seller may think I'm really serious and know, to the dollar, what to offer. The truth is I randomly made up the number in a few seconds, but it makes it look like I thought about it for hours.

I told him my offer, and he accepted it a day or two later. He said the offers were close, but I beat them out, and he also liked the fact that I was a real estate agent. I could write the contract for him and help with title companies, and he would not have to worry about all that.

Many people assume that being an agent hurts on off-market deals. I do have to disclose that I am an agent and even disclose that I may make a profit and might not be paying full-market-value for the property. However, being an agent can also have its advantages.

I am licensed with the state of Colorado, and it is very easy for people to find me if I decide to rip someone off and try to disappear. There is a very simple and easy way to file a complaint against me if I act unethically. I can show people that I have been in business for years without complaints and that I am not going anywhere. I can also take care of the paperwork and know how to do things the right way.

One of the biggest risks of selling real estate without real estate agents involved is not doing the paperwork correctly. The contract may not include everything it should, or something may not have been clear. Both sides cannot agree on what was agreed upon, resulting in a lawsuit. The fact that the contract is about 20 pages long is a pain, but there is a reason for it, and in the end, it helps account for every possibility and avoid lawsuits.

So, I got this property under contract and decided to line up financing! I know many people line up financing before they get deals under contract, and that is the smart thing to do for most people. However, I have a number of lending sources and could pay cash if I really had to.

I ended up using the local portfolio lender I used to finance many of my residential rentals. They offered me ARMs on my residential rentals with 30-year amortizations, but on my commercial rental, they would only do a 15-year fixed-rate loan.

I prefer 30-year loans because of the lower payments, which means I can increase my cash flow and invest more money now. I make a lot more than the 4 or 5 percent rate on the loans, so I don't worry about paying them off early, especially since I usually have plenty of equity.

This was a small loan (75% of the $101,250 purchase price), so I was okay with the 15-year term.

The property needed some work, but was a concrete block building with very little inside. It had been used as a livestock feed store for many years. We painted the exterior, cleaned up the interior, and put it up for rent. I think we spent $10,000 or less on the rehab.

I had Nikki handle the rental process and property management. She has done property management in the past and knew what to do, although property management is not her favorite thing. We have property managers on our residential properties, but they are not qualified to rent out commercial properties, and I wanted to handle the renting of these commercial properties in the beginning to see how it went.

She was able to get it rented out fairly quickly by posting adds on Zillow and Craigslist and by mentioning it on Facebook. This was before Facebook Marketplace, so we did not have that option. We asked $1,500 a month with the tenants paying utilities. We still would take care of the exterior maintenance, taxes, and insurance, so it would be considered a modified gross lease. I don't think I was even familiar with NNN leases at the time.

Nikki received an inquiry from a traffic control company, and she was familiar with the tenants. She grew up in a fairly small town in Northern Colorado. Two brothers owned the company, and she knew one of them a little bit. We checked their references, which turned out to be great. They had never rented commercial space before, but they had rented properties for a while, and their landlords said they were awesome tenants. They had decent credit and no other issues.

They moved in and paid rent for a few months before the problems started. A few neighbors complained that the brothers were always fighting in the parking lot—not just arguing, but physically fighting. The neighbors never called the cops, and we did not have much to go on besides the neighbors' reports. We told the neighbors to call the cops if the fights turned serious, and we would talk to the tenants.

After talking to the tenants, it was clear the brothers had some personal issues, but they said they understood the problem and would be more mindful of the neighbors. The company they ran was in charge of directing traffic for construction zones. I always thought the city did that kind of work, but I guess outside companies handle traffic control as well.

A couple months went by. They paid their rent, and then one brother called. He said he wanted his other brother off the lease. They had a falling out and were not working together anymore. This was not a good sign. We reminded the brother that they both signed the lease and were both liable for any damages or problems. One brother could not simply take the other off the lease.

A few months later, the rent stopped coming in, and more drama ensued. I won't tell you exactly what they told us about the falling out since it's very sensitive information I am sure they wanted to keep to themselves. I can't remember for sure, but I know at least one of the brothers ended up in jail. They stopped returning calls, so we were forced to move forward with an eviction.

I had always thought a commercial eviction was easier than a residential one, but our lawyers informed us we would have to go through the courts and it would take 6 weeks. We went through that process, gained possession of the property, and saw what the place looked like.

It was pretty trashed, but again, it was a concrete-block building with very little to no damage. There was a bathroom and one little office inside. They had put holes in the interior office walls, left a ton of trash, and even some illegal items.

They also left behind many of traffic cones and things we could use! Those tenants cost us about $10,000 in court fees, lawyers, lost rent, and cleanup, but it could have been much worse.

We cleaned up the place and rented it out again a couple of months later for $1,500 a month to a welding company. That welding company has been in the building over a year now and has been great.

Knock on wood—that experience was the worst we have had with commercial tenants. Our other tenants have been fantastic because they run a business out of the property, and that is their livelihood.

This property is worth well more than $200,000 now, and I will show you how we know that based on the next case study.

23

Case Study #4: One of My Best Deals Ever

Rental Property #20

This was supposed to be my first commercial rental property. I talked about it earlier in the book as the property that helped get me into commercial real estate. I found it on the MLS in the beginning of 2017. It was listed for $110,000.

I could not believe how cheap it was, and that was the only reason I considered it. If it had been $150,000, I would have passed it right over. However, it was hard to find any properties for $150,000—or even $200,000—at the time. When I saw the price, I knew I had to take a look at it.

It was occupied by a furniture refinishing business and was being used as a retail space and workshop. The listing agent insisted he be present during the showing. With residential properties, the buyer's agent can almost always show them on their own. You don't need the listing agent present. However, with commercial properties, the listing agent almost always wants to be present.

The property looked to be in decent shape, and it was over 3,000 square feet. Plus, it had an unfinished basement for more storage that was not included in the square footage. After seeing the property, I knew it was a good deal. When I made the offer, I had not yet bought my other commercial rentals, but it was so cheap and so big I could not pass it up.

I sent a full-price offer to the listing agent. He asked me if it was correct since I was offering full price on a property that had only been on the market 2 days. I would later realize how long closing a commercial deal takes and why my full-price offer was so surprising.

The seller accepted my offer, and then I had to wait. I had written into the contract a 30-day close. However, some tax issues had to be cleared up, and although I wrote the offer in January, we did not close until November! I stuck it out and eventually got the deal done, but that is why this was the first commercial rental that caught my eye yet the fourth one I actually purchased!

For financing, I used private money. I have a private-money lender who often lends me money on house flips and was happy to lend on this property as well. My plan was to use private money to buy the property, get it rented out, and then refinance with a traditional bank.

When I first got the property under contract, the occupant was the owner. H said he planned to move to a new facility but may want to rent the place back from me for a short while. I thought that would be fantastic and told him he could rent it for $1,500 a month. I guess $1,500 is my going rate.

He agreed and signed a six-month lease. I started talking to lenders about refinancing it, and they all wanted me to own it a year before they would let me take cash out. I decided to wait and hope the tenant would stay longer than he planned.

When we got close to that six months, I talked to the tenant, and he was still happy, so we agreed to extend the lease another year. Once I had that year-long lease in place, I started to talk to lenders again, and they were now more willing to refinance it.

I talked to the lender who had refinanced rental number 18, and they were interested in doing this one as well. The appraisal came in at $250,000! I could not believe it was that high, even though the numbers could be manipulated to make it that high.

The rent was $1,500 a month or $18,000 a year. If you take that income and divide it by a 7% cap rate, you get a value of $257,142.85. Our area supports a 7% cap rate all day long, but the reason I was surprised by this value is CAP rate is supposed to be based on the net income, not gross income. That $18,000 a year is the gross income. I was paying property taxes, insurance, and outside maintenance, which costs me some money. The taxes for this property were a couple thousand a year at the time. I think our insurance was over $1,000 a year as well. If the actual income was $14,000 a year, the value would be $200,000 at a 7% CAP rate.

I think the appraisal came in high, which hardly ever happens, because the property is rented out a little cheaper than it should be based on how large it is. It really could be rented for close to $2,000 a month with the perfect tenant, but that would take some work and kicking out this tenant.

I got the refinance done with a new loan of $175,000 (70% of value). It had a ten-year term. The amortization was 25 years, and the fixed term was 7 years. I was able to cash out $70,000 more than I bought the property for. This was the classic BRRRR strategy on a commercial property: Buy, Repair (although it needed almost nothing), Rent, Refinance, and Repeat (which I tend to do). To be honest, if I was tight on cash and dependent on this cash flow, I would have really tight cash-flow numbers.

My payment on this without taxes and insurance is about $1,000 a month. Plus, we have around $400 a month in taxes and insurance we have to pay now. That means I am only making $100 a month with no other costs!

I would not suggest buying rentals that result in numbers that tight. So why did I do it? I have plenty of cash in reserves, and I do not depend on this property to make me money. I also think we could rent it out for more if we ever lose the tenant. If we earned $2,000 a month, we would be making decent money with a great ratio.

I even told the lender I would be happy doing a lower loan amount, but they really wanted to do the 70%. I was certainly happy to take all that cash out and have the appraiser and lender confirm this was a really good deal when I bought it!

The other issue I want to talk about with this property is the repairs. I mentioned BRRRR, which usually involves residential rentals and repairing them to add value. I am able to add value to commercial properties without repairing them in many cases.

Maybe I need to change the BRRRR strategy to the BRRR strategy: Buy, Rent, Refinance, Repeat. I love buying properties and adding value without having to spend money on repairs, although that rarely happens.

With this property, we did have to make some repairs. However, they came up as we owned the property...not right away. The biggest thing we had to do was replace the roof. Many online sources and landlords talk about replacing roofs and how expensive it is. However, that is not always the case.

We live in Colorado, where we get a lot of hail. Hail damage is covered by insurance. The tenants in this building complained about the roof leaking about a year after I bought it. our roofers inspected it and found it was in pretty bad shape and had hail damage, which insurance might cover.

The insurance company inspected it and confirmed the hail damage. They told us they would pay somewhere around $12,000 for a new roof. I was happy the insurance would pay for the roof, but it was going to cost more than $12,000. This was a 3,000-square-foot building with both a sloped and flat roof.

Our roofer said it would take $17,000 to get this roof repaired the right way. Luckily the insurance company's first offer is not always the last amount they will pay. Our roofing company called the insurance company, discussed the situation, and got our payout raised to $17,000 minus our $1,000 deductible.

We had a brand new roof for only $1,000! We also spent $2,000 on the HVAC system, and besides that, we have not had to make any repairs. The tenant has covered everything else they needed.

While commercial properties usually take less money to maintain than residential properties, especially with NNN leases, they do take some money. You have to be prepared to pay out some cash for maintenance or tenant improvements if you have to re-lease.

As you can see, having to make a few repairs along the way can be well worth it when you buy right! This property is still rented to the furniture-restoration business.

24

Case Study #5: $2 Million? Was I Ready?

Rental property #21

This is going to be a long chapter because this is the craziest and best investment I have ever made. It is also the biggest and most expensive property I have ever purchased.

I had been looking for a large commercial deal to buy for many years. Even before I started buying smaller commercial deals, I wanted to buy a large warehouse of some sort, split it up into smaller spaces, and rent out those spaces. I looked at a few buildings, but the process and price was daunting. The renovation costs and timeframes were also intimidating.

Then, this property showed up. It was brought to me by a commercial broker who I had tried to do some deals with in the past. I had used this broker to make offers for me on other properties. Even though I am an agent, I knew I did not know enough about commercial real estate to do it all on my own, at least with big properties.

The broker told me about a few deals he wanted to show me. The deal I ended up buying was the most exciting to me, but before we saw that one, he showed me another big property.

The property was located in Greeley, Colorado where I live and where most of my business is done. It was downtown and had 50,000 square feet plus a basement with 20,000 more square feet.

It was very cheap for the size, with an asking price of about $3,500,000. That is about $70 a square foot for the main level when most properties were selling for $100 a square foot or more.

This property was a three-story office building with retail space on the main floor. It was near a lot of downtown foot traffic. Downtown sounds great, but the Greeley's downtown has struggled for many years. It is doing better now, but the problem is most of the new development in town is about 5 miles west.

I was not sure that I liked the idea of a downtown property. Yes, the area was doing better, but it could also get worse again very quickly. The other problem I had with the building was the tenants and the layout.

The property was mostly office space with multiple units. I think there are something like 28 different spaces, and many of them were vacant. There were some good tenants, some bad tenants, some long leases, and some month-to-month leases. There was a new coffee shop on the main floor and much vacant space on the main floor.

The owner of the building was a commercial broker, and his office was in the building. His job was basically to manage those tenants, and he was having problems finding enough tenants. That really worried me for a couple of reasons:

1. Why was he having so many problems finding tenants when he worked there and was there all the time?

2. How much work would it take me to find new tenants and get this property stabilized?

Then another problem popped up: parking. The building had a footprint of 18,000 square feet—the size of the main floor, which took up the entire lot—and the only parking available was on the street or a public lot next to it.

Both the brokers who told me about this property and the owner were sure the city was going to approve a new parking garage in the public lot right next to the building, but nothing had been approved yet. There was already a parking problem in the area, and that is why the parking garage was being proposed. There was a two-hour limit for parking on the streets and in most public lots, so people who worked downtown had to constantly move their cars if they did not have private parking.

After thinking about these issues, I decided to pass, and so did my partner.

Yes, I brought a partner in with me to look at these deals. These were multi-million dollar properties, and I was not sure I could pull it off on my own or if the banks would lend to me on my own. My partner had more commercial experience and a lot of cash.

The best deal ever

The next property we looked at was the one I was really interested in. This property was within two blocks of where I worked. It was a 68,000-square-foot commercial strip mall with over 4 acres.

It had a grocery store, which took up most of the space using 52,000 square feet. There was also a restaurant occupying about 5,000 square feet and a small office that used 1,600 square feet. That left about 9,000 square feet of vacant space.

The vacant space had been used as a thrift store and office space. There was also a land lease for a coffee shop. On a land lease, the tenant owns the building and can take it if they want.

They were asking $2,250,000 for the property, which seemed like a steal to me. I had seen quite a few properties for sale in the area, and there were some big properties with prices similar to this one. There was a 60,000-square-foot building that sold for $2,500,000. There was also a 250,000-square-foot building I had under contract for $2,500,000.

Both of those properties were vacant and had been for years. They needed hundreds of thousands or millions of dollars in rehab to get them rent ready. It might take years to fix them up and get them leased. On properties that are vacant and need work, it is also very tough to get financing. I was very interested in those properties, and I think they were great deals for the right buyer, but I am also glad I did not buy them knowing what I know now!

The great part about this property was it was big, had a lot of land, was in a great location, and was mostly rented. On top of that, it was super cheap!

My partner and I saw it and decided we needed to buy it. The agent who brought it to me was acting as a transaction broker and was both my agent and the sellers agent. This is always a tricky situation because you are not technically supposed to work for either party's best interests, but it is hard not to.

This was a very good price, and we were strongly encouraged to offer full price. We decided to offer $2,000,000 to see what the seller would say. I used that agent to help with the technicalities and help me get deals, but I still had control of the offer. We made the offer and waited.

This was where I began to learn patience in the commercial real estate world. On residential deals, I was used to getting my offers accepted, countered, or declined in a day or two. Expect to wait weeks for a response on bigger commercial deals.

We did wait weeks, and then, the seller gave us a counter for $2,100,000. I was pretty happy with that number, and after talking to my partner, we decided to go for it and accepted the deal.

This is another reason I was glad to have a commercial broker on my side. The timelines are so much different on commercial deals than they are on residential. On a residential deal, I may close in 3 weeks or less.

I think we had 120 days to close this deal, and we had 90 days for the inspection, 110 days to get the loan, and longer on the other dates. I would have had no clue how to set those dates on my own and would have never thought we would have had that much time to get it all done.

Under Contract

So, we had the deal under contract, and I had to provide $50,000 in earnest money. That is a lot of money, but in Colorado, it is very hard to lose your earnest money. If we cancel due to the loan, inspection, insurance or any of the other contingencies written into the contract falling apart, and we tell them by the date we list in the contract we are cancelling, we get our earnest money back. So, it was not like we were out that money.

We had to get to work on this property. We needed to get a loan, complete an inspection, and go through the appraisal. I guess it was good to have so much time do all of this since I had never done a deal this size before.

The first thing we did was find an inspector. I asked the commercial agent if he could recommend anyone, and he gave us a few names. This was a huge building, and with larger buildings comes higher inspection costs! I experienced some sticker shock when I saw it was going to cost us over $4,000. I was used to inspections costing $300 or less (even $0), since I rarely ordered residential inspections.

This was a big deal, a lot of money, and a complicated property. It was built in the 1960s, and we decided we better get an inspection to see what kind of shape everything was in. The nice part was an environmental phase 1 report had already been done.

Wondering what a phase 1 report is? Well, I didn't know either. Many big commercial properties have environmental reports done to see if there are any hazardous materials present. There could be lead-based paint, asbestos, underground storage tanks, or some other chemical contamination.

To be honest, if I had not been told there was an environmental report on the property already, I would never have thought of getting one. The only thing that may have come up was our lender may have asked for one.

The environmental report showed no problems. That was great news, but I have never been as scared as others about those things as I possibly should be. I know they can be dangerous if disturbed, and we have always been careful and abide by local guidelines to remove those items when needed, but I would probably have still done this deal if it did have asbestos or lead-based paint.

We agreed to the price and waited for the inspection to be completed. I think it took a few weeks before the results came back. Only a few things caught our eye.

The electrical seemed to be in good shape, as did the plumbing and HVAC. One really cool thing about this building was the grocery store maintained and repaired everything in their space and even in their part of the parking lot. Their rent was super cheap, which I will explain soon, but they paid for the roof if it needed work, paid for the parking lot if it needed to be resurfaced, and had recently spent $300,000 refurbishing the interior and exterior of their portion of the building.

The big issue we found was the roof, which was flat, like most large commercial buildings. Most of the roof had been redone in the last 20 years, and those roofs are supposed to last 50 years if well maintained. It was a rubber-membrane with some rooftop HVAC units.

The back of the building had a raised roof because part of the back had a 2nd story. This square footage was not included in the 68,000. It is always nice to find bonus square feet in buildings!

The raised portion of the roof was not in great shape. It was old, cracking, and leaking. We had a roofing company inspect it, and they said fixing it correctly would cost at least $50,000. Other minor issues on the report didn't worry me, and the commercial agent seemed to think they gave us some leverage.

I think we asked for a $120,000 price reduction the repairs, which was more than my gut told me to ask for. We waited for weeks for a response and were told that was not an unreasonable request. When we finally got a response, we were told the seller was pissed off and wanted to cancel the entire deal. He said he was already selling at a discount and was pretty offended we wanted even more off the price.

I can't say I disagree with that opinion. After some work, a lot of communication, and some honesty, we got the seller to continue with the deal with no reduction on sales price. We got nothing, but to me that was okay because it was a great deal.

We were being greedy, and it almost backfired big time. I should have known better. On residential deals, I always preach not to ask for too much from the seller or they may get offended and give you nothing or cancel the deal. It is better to be fair and ask for only major items to be fixed or for a reasonable credit. I did not follow my own rules.

Thankfully, we kept the deal going, and it makes me sick to my stomach to think that we almost lost it because of that inspection request.

The next step was getting the appraisal and loan. I think we had been working on finding a lender while the inspection was going on, but we had not finalized anything.

We talked to a few lenders about doing this deal, and all of them seemed excited when we mentioned it. They thought it was a great price and a great property. We told them what terms we were looking for, and they did not seem to think they were unreasonable terms.

We wanted 75% loan to value, which is pretty common with commercial properties, but you can sometimes go up to 80%. We wanted a 25 year amortization, which seemed reasonable. We were looking for fixed rates under 5% and at least a ten-year term.

We submitted our applications, and my partner and I had worked with all of them previously and already held loans with them. When the time came to give us actual approval on the terms, the stories changed quickly.

One of the most disappointing things I have found with commercial rentals is working with banks. Numerous times with numerous banks, I have been told that refinancing or getting loans would be no problem, but when it comes down to getting the loan, all the terms change or the deal is suddenly too risky. We then have to find a new bank, which takes much more time, not to mention having to submit new applications.

Two banks said they would do the deal but only for 15 years or 5-year term. On a deal this size, we did not want to have to refinance after 5 years, even though we are refinancing much sooner than that. More on that later.

Even though a couple of banks changed the terms, we found a bank that would do the deal we wanted. Now, we had to get an appraisal. Some banks even changed their story after the appraisal.

When we ordered the appraisal, we experienced sticker shock again. The appraisal cost more than $4,000. We ordered the appraisal after getting the inspection issues sorted out, which pushed our time frames. I thought we would have plenty of time, but it takes so long to get things done in commercial that we were pushing our deadlines.

In fact, we needed an extension from the seller for the appraisal. This is another reason he was not happy with us because this was happening as we were having our dispute about the inspection requests. He could have easily denied our request to extend the dates for the appraisal and killed the deal.

We got it sorted out, and the appraisal was ordered. I did not think there would be a problem with the appraisal because we were getting the property so cheap. I was right.

The appraisal came back at $2,400,000. I almost never see an appraisal come back for more than the contract price, especially significantly more than the contract price. The appraiser even told me he was having a hard time coming in with a value that low. He could not believe we were getting the property so cheap.

I thought we were getting an amazing deal as well, but there is always that suspicion in the back of your head that comes with a great deal. What are you missing? What is wrong with the property? I am usually pretty good about ignoring those thoughts, but it was nice to have outside verification that we got a great deal.

We bought the property in February, 2018, and my partner and I each brought half the money for closing, which was a lot—25% of $2,100,000, which is $575,000 plus the closing costs. We paid .5% origination fees to the bank along with closing fees, upfront interest, insurance, and a bunch of little costs. We each had to bring about $300,000 into the deal.

Getting this done took a lot of work, stress, and time, but it was all worth it and was the best deal I have ever done, as you'll see in part 2 of this case study.

25

Case Study #5 Part 2: Adding Millions in Value

This is a big property, so I am dedicating a big part of this book to it. Buying the property was just the beginning. A lot has happened since as far as adding valuing and turning my life upside down...but in a good way.

First, we need to talk a little bit about the numbers and why this was such a great deal. I have mentioned the size and the appraisal, but what about the rents?

While there was some vacant space in the building and the grocery store was not paying fair market value for rent, it was still a fantastic deal. We bought it at around a 9% CAP rate. A 6 or 7% CAP rate seems to be the norm in my area. A 9% CAP rate is a smoking deal and what you would expect for a vacant property that needs work, not a property that is in pretty good shape and has tenants, even if it is not 100% full.

When we bought this property, it had about $20,000 in gross rents coming in from NNN leases. As a reminder, an NNN lease means the tenants pay most of the expenses. In this case, the grocery store paid for everything directly for their part of the building and the other tenants paid NNN fees to the landlords who then paid the property taxes, insurance, management, and other fees.

The NNN fess the tenants paid did not quite add up to the actual NNN costs. The landlord often estimates the NNN costs at the beginning of the lease, and those costs can go up or down based on the actual costs. However, there is often a clause that says the NNN costs cannot increase more than a certain amount.

With this building, the tenants were paying too little for the NNN costs, and the leases stipulated the NNN could only be raised 5% a year. The landlords had to pay additional expenses because of this and some vacant units

With a fully leased building on NNN leases, all the maintenance and utility expenses should be paid by the tenants. However, vacancies lead to fewer tenants to pay the share of NNN costs and utilities.

After taking into account the extra costs and utilities the landlords were paying, the property was generating about $17,000 a month, which bring. That means we bought the property at just over a 9% CAP rate, which is amazing in our market.

Our loan payments were about $10,500 a month, resulting in $6,500 after all expenses and accounting for two vacant units. We were making 13% profits after paying the mortgage and the extra expenses. That assumes we put $600,000 into the property for down payments and all of the other costs.

While this was a great deal, it got much better.

The first thing that blew my mind was how much of the loan we paid off monthly. Our payment was over $10,000, but we paid off about $4,000 a month. That resulted in a return that adds 8% to the 13%.

The mortgage pay down is not money in our pocket, but it is adding a lot of equity every month. That was a cool thing to see, but that wasn't all.

I mentioned that this building turned my life upside down. The reason I say that is I decided it was the perfect time to start my own office. I had worked at Pro Realty for 16 years as a real estate agent. My dad had helped start the office back in 1992, and although he no longer had any ownership in the office and was retired, I had never considered moving to another brokerage. I had considered starting my own office a few times.

When I was at Pro, I had a pretty big team. I had a couple of assistants, an agent or two, and we took up two or three offices. I paid a lot of money to that office and had always wanted to start my own.

The reason I had never started one was my primary business for many years was as a HUD and REO listing broker. I listed foreclosures for banks and the government. At one point, I was selling 200 properties a year all over the state.

I loved selling foreclosures, but the agreement I had with most of the banks was that the government went through my broker. Technically, most of my listings were listed with my broker, and then he designated me as the person to handle all of the work. I found those clients, talked to them, and 95% of them had no idea who my broker was, but that was how they did business. That meant if I started an office, there was no guarantee those accounts would come with me. They might, but then again, they might not, and I was not willing to take that risk.

Things changed in Colorado in 2015: foreclosures disappeared. That meant I was no longer getting very many REO or HUD listings. I would get listings here and there, but by 2018, I was getting almost nothing. I had no reason not to start my own office.

I decided, with the new building, I would start my own brokerage and bring my team with me (or at least I assumed they would come with me). The building had vacant space, and I wanted to start an office. It seemed like a perfect fit.

I talked to my partner, and we agreed to rent 4,500 square feet of the vacant space to me. We decided on a fair but discounted rental rate (this was probably a mistake in the long run). I decided that I would start my office in a few months.

My life was turned upside down because I decided to do the right thing and tell my broker the plan. I had a few offices, and I knew it would hurt him when I left. I told him, when I was buying the building, I might start my own office, but I don't think he believed me. After I bought the building, I told him again, and the plan was to leave June 1st.

He seemed surprised. I continued with my plan and thought I had a few months to get everything together and get the office fixed up a little bit. I was wrong.

A couple weeks later, my broker asked me to see him about some files. It turns out I had bought some deals from wholesalers, and no lead-based-paint disclosures had been signed. On every deal, lead-based-paint disclosures should be signed to inform the buyer that a property built prior to 1978 may or may not have lead-based paint.

Wholesalers often use their own contracts. We had not involved agents in these deals since I was buying them for myself, and I had overlooked that lead-based-paint disclosures should be signed.

Was this my fault? Yes. I take full responsibly. Was this a big deal? Well, it was a big enough deal for my broker to fire me. He said I had 10 days to figure out what to do and vacate the office.

I was shocked. I thought I was doing my broker a favor by telling him I was leaving ahead of time, but it turned out I should have kept it a secret until the very end. My broker also informed me he had contacted the EPA (environmental protection agency) and the Colorado real estate commission.

I freaked out for a second thinking I was going to lose my license and get into all kinds of trouble. What did I do? I called the Realtor hotline, which gives me access to attorneys who are well versed in real estate law.

I talked to an attorney, told my story, and asked how much trouble I was in. He told me in lawyer talk, which means I am trying to give you advice without admitting or specifically giving advice, that there was no problem.

He said what I did was not disclose to myself that there could be lead-based paint. Yes, technically I should have had disclosures signed, but the only person harmed was me. He said he could not imagine how the real estate commission would care, and he said the EPA definitely didn't care. I was more than relieved, and I was annoyed at my broker.

It also did not change the fact that I had ten days to move to a new brokerage or start my own. Luckily, I had been proactive and already taken my managing broker classes, and I was more than qualified.

I spent the next two days applying for the license, but I needed an office to manage. I had to create that office and company as well. I am very fortunate that I had an and still have an amazing team, including Nikki, who helped me get all of this together.

Of course, the biggest question was what to call it. After brainstorming and polling many people, mostly my team and family, we came up with Blue Steel Real Estate.

Yes, that has connections to the movie Zoolander, which is one of my all-time favorite movies. I also own two blue cars: a 1999 Lamborghini Diablo and a 1998 Lotus Esprit. My favorite color is blue, and I get made fun of on a regular basis for regularly wearing blue polos.

Within a few days, the real estate commission approved my new office, and I was a managing broker. Now where do I go? Luckily the new building had not one vacant space but two! I wanted to remodel the main space where our office would be. It would be really hard to move into that space while it was being remodeled.

We moved into the old thrift-store space, which was not amazing by any standards, but it had walls, bathrooms, carpet, and a big open room. The next few days was a whirlwind of moving files, desks, computers, getting the internet hooked up, getting phones going, changing all our marketing, and moving our listings over.

We stayed in that space for a few months while we remodeled the other vacant unit. Some of my team didn't come with me. Justin, one of my best friends from college who had been with me for years stayed at Pro. He stayed there for about a month to help us transition, and then he came to our company!

We planned to be in the new space on June 1st, but with construction delays and losing one contractor in the process, it was the middle of June. A few more agents who were not on my team came over from Pro as well.

We had added about $2,000 a month in rent to the building and had reduced multiple expenses because utilities were being paid for by that tenant. Also, more NNN costs were coming in. By moving into my own building, I added about $450,000 in value based on a 7% CAP rate.

Adding another tenant

We still had a vacant unit. The unit I moved into had been vacant for years. It was listed for lease, but it was a mess, with cubicles falling apart, broken ceiling tiles all over, and trash everywhere. I could see why it had not rented for all those years. The other space had a tenant recently, but it was ugly as well.

It had become even uglier because we moved many of the unwanted cubicles and desks into that space while we remodeled the space for my office. We tried to give away all of it, and only a small fraction disappeared. We listed it for rent, but I was not getting any action.

The property was still doing great because I added a tenant and had reduced expenses. The old landlord had used a property management who charged $400 a month just to handle maintenance and repairs. I could do that myself for less money and already had the contractors to do all the work for less money.

I still wanted to get that space leased out. Something I learned through all of this is that it is not always what you know but who you know. The local commercial brokers have a monthly meeting at different locations, and I got an email saying they needed a space on short notice. I agreed to host at my new office.

We catered the meeting, and since I was the host, I was able to pitch my building. It worked—at least I think it worked. A number of people inquired about the space in a month's time.

Before I get into the new inquiries, I should mention that the broker who sold me the property had a tenant who wanted the space from the beginning. A laundromat wanted to move in, but the terms made me question why some landlords do what they do.

The laundromat wanted us to remodel the space for them and add massive water taps, and they wanted to pay bottom-of-the-barrel lease rates. I could not understand why anyone would take them up on this offer because it would take 10 years to get our money back through rent.

My partner could not understand it either, but I guess if you were going to sell the building soon or refinance it, the added rent would increase the value of the building enough to make it worthwhile to some investors. It was not to me.

The first potential tenant who approached me wanted to start an event center. I was interested in this plan, but it quickly lost its charm after I learned a few things:

1. They wanted a liquor license, and the lease for the restaurant stated no other liquor licenses would be granted to tenants in the building.
2. They had no experience with event centers. This would be their first venture.
3. They wanted at least $50,000 in tenant improvements paid for by the landlord.
4. They changed brokers.

At first, this tenant was talking to me about all of their plans. I met them at the building, talked to them multiple times, and then they said I need to talk to their broker because they felt they needed help. Now I would have to pay a commission to another broker if they signed a lease.

To put the icing on the cake, guess who was their new broker—my old broker at pro Realty.

I tried to keep my feelings out of it and think of it as a purely business decision, but getting fired is hard to ignore, so a new tenant entered the picture.

I believe the new tenant came from an agent that was at my broker meeting. That broker's daughter helped run a dance studio and wanted a new space. I was intrigued by the dance studio from the beginning. They had many things going for them:

1. They had been in business for 30 years.
2. They needed tenant finishes, but they were less than the other potential tenants.
3. My daughter loves to dance!

We received letter of intent from both the dance studio and event center after getting nothing for almost a year. I decided to go with the dance studio.

We signed a lease for $8.75 a square foot with the tenant paying NNN costs. We had a few months to transform the vacant unit from a crappy office to a modern inviting space.

I think something that helped the dance studio choose our space was something extremely selfish and fun we did. In the back of the empty space, we built a golf simulator right before all of the interest in the vacant space. We took out the ceiling tiles to give us more height, painted everything black, and made it look pretty good for little money. The dance studio saw the ceiling height and what could be done, and they loved it.

Something I have said before is that showing what a space can look like really helps it rent. It does not have to be perfect, but it should not be trashed.

When we did this remodel, the dance studio asked for a CO (Certificate of Occupancy). We talked to the city, and they said it should be no problem.

When it came time to call the city, they said the dance studio was a change of use and we needed to pull a full building permit. We had not done any structural work, and anything we added needed to be up to code, but this still worried us as the city suddenly became very tough to work with. We had to give them a list of contractors we used, including electricians and plumbers, even if no electrical work or plumbing work was done. We got our list together, and the city scheduled their inspection. They walked through the space in about 2 minutes, left, and approved us. It appeared as though they just wanted their $4,000 inspection fee.

We spent about $40,000 on the rehab for the dance studio. They moved in, and we added about $3,500 a month in rent and expenses, adding $600,000 in value to the property based on a 7% CAP rate.

The new numbers

After adding the new leases, we had added about $1,000,000 in value based on a 7% CAP rate. I was pretty happy about this. However, we also got an amazing deal on this property. I think we bought it for almost one million dollars less than it was worth in the first place. Of course, all of this is hypothetical since we have not tried to sell the property or refinance it yet.

While we owned the property, rent was also increasing for the existing tenants. You will find that most good commercial leases will have escalating rent clauses. That means every year, or every few years, the rent increases. This was the case with this property, and the grocery store, small office, and restaurant all saw rent increases while we owned the property.

With all said and done, we had about $26,000 a month in rent coming in plus fewer expenses because the new tenants were paying NNN costs and their share of the utilities. Instead of making $6,500 a month after paying the mortgage, we were now making close to $15,000 a month after paying the mortgage.

Based on a 7% CAP rate, here is what the building should be worth:

- $25,000 a month income equaling $300,000 a year (remember the mortgage expense is not included when calculating the value of the property).
- $300,000 / 7% CAP rate equals $4,285,000

Theoretically, conservatively the property is worth more than $4,000,000 with a 7% CAP rate!

After paying down the loan for more than a year, we owed less than $1,500,000 and had $2,500,000 in equity from a $600,000 initial investment. We had also been making money every month. That's not bad for my first big commercial deal.

One reason I don't like having partners is I do not have complete control of the investment, or I may have explain why I do some of the things I do. My partner on this property is awesome, which is why I was comfortable working with him. He provided input on the deal and helped with many things, but he has also been cool with letting me make most of the decisions and handle the leases. He also understood when I took over property management that I would be paid extra on top of the returns we are getting for all the work I was doing.

One thing my partner and I disagree on is debt and how to handle it. I prefer to use debt to build my empire and keep growing. He likes to pay off debt and is much more conservative. I cannot argue with him too much because he has been very successful over the years.

With this building, I saw all that equity and thought about how many more properties I could buy with it. He, on the other hand, was thinking about how fast we could pay the loan off if we used all the cash flow we were making to apply to the loan.

Luckily, my partner is very cool and saw how far his investment had gone without much work on his part. I had made him a lot of money, but he brought a lot to the table since I do not know if I could have done this deal without him. If I had used a different partner, I am sure there would have been much push back on how things should be done and more looking over my shoulder to make sure it was all done right.

After some discussion, he agreed that refinancing and pulling cash out made sense. We started talking to banks about getting a new loan that would replace the old loan and put a lot of tax-free money in our pockets .

26

Case Study #5 Part 3: BRRR on a Big Scale

I've successfully refinanced other properties before. I ran into some problems, and one of those problems involved the bank that financed this big property. I had wanted to refinance rental property number 18. The appraisal was completed, and after the appraisal they changed all the terms on me! I was not happy about that, but I found another bank that worked with me and got the right terms in place.

We talked to this bank again about refinancing this property, and they really wanted to be the bank that got the loan. I sat down with the banker before we started the process, and I told him the terms we wanted and told him I wanted to make sure his bank could do it.

I wanted a 75% loan-to-value mortgage based on a new appraisal. We wanted at least a 20-year amortization, if not 25 years , and a 10-year term. We also wanted a good rate. He expressed some reservation about being able to do the full 75% since we would be taking so much cash out. He said his bank would want to know what the money was being used for and all the costs we incurred leasing the property.

I told him a few times what we used the money for didn't really matter in my mind, but we would be using it to buy more properties, and we might spend some more money on the exterior as the restaurant facade was beginning to age. I said I needed a firm commitment on a 75% loan before we moved forward.

He called me back and said they could do the 75%, at least a 20-year amortization, a rate close to what we had now, which was 4.6%, a ten-year term, and .5% origination fee on the new part of the loan (additional money being lent over and above what we already had borrowed from them).

That sounded good to me, and my partner was good with it as well. We asked to get the appraisal ordered first and get moving.

The lender handles ordering the appraisal, and he gave us two choices. 1) We could have an appraiser complete the report in a month for $8,000, or we could have a different appraiser complete it for $4,000 in 8 weeks. We went with the eight-week option because we were not in a huge hurry.

After at least 8 weeks, the appraiser called to set up an inspection on the property. He showed up, and I walked him through the building. He was very nice and said we got an awesome deal on the property and thought, off hand, it was worth anywhere from $3,000,000 to $5,000,000, but he had not dug into the numbers yet.

He asked us to send him all the financial reports, which we did for every month since the purchase. We waited around another few weeks and got the appraisal back. It came in at $3,500,000. That was okay...but less than I was hoping for. After all the numbers I ran, I thought it was conservatively worth at least $4,000,000.

Since I can be a diligent and stubborn SOB, I asked to see the appraisal so I could figure out how the value came in so low. FYI—if you want to see the numbers and my analysis of the appraisal, there's a video on the InvestFourMore YouTube channel. Just search for InvestFourMore and "appraisal."

I dug into the numbers and found multiple issues right away. The appraisal had been completed using a mix of income, replacement value, and comparable-sales value. The appraiser looked at what the income said it was worth, what comparable sales said it was worth, and what the building replacement cost would be.

This property is located on the busiest street in the town, and I think it is a fantastic location. The appraiser used comparable sales that were on cul-de-sacs miles away! He also compared it to much-smaller properties that sold for similar prices but then made huge deductions on our property because it was older.

He also compared it to a Sears store that had recently been sold after being vacant for a few years. That store was bigger than ours but vacant with no income coming in. It was torn down shortly after we got the appraisal, and it turns out it was purchased by the main guy who used to own all Sears stores. It was not an arms-length transaction, which means a fair-market sale where the seller and buyer do not know each other. It was basically bought by the guy who sold it.

For the replacement costs, the appraiser said the building was only worth $3,000,000, which is a joke. This building would cost $8 million to rebuild according to my insurance agent, and that is after we worked really hard to get that value down as far as we could. Even with depreciation and deferred maintenance, this building is worth $5 million plus based on replacement costs.

For the income portion of the valuation, the appraiser said the property was worth $2,800,000 based on the income excluding the land lease. The land lease brought in $2,500 a month, and he valued that separately. He was saying the building without the land lease was making $167,000 a year or

$14,000 a month. I could not figure out where he got this number. We were making $25,000 a month, and even if we took out the $2,500 for the land lease, we were at $22,500 a month. If you counted multiple expenses the tenants pretty much paid, it was still almost impossible to get down to that number. One cool fact was the appraiser valued the property at a 5.9% CAP rate, which was lower than I thought it would be by a long shot. The lower the cap rat,e the more valuable the property.

I expressed my concerns to the banker. The banker was not very helpful. He kept telling me he thought it was a decent number and did not see any issues. In hindsight, I think he was working to get that number lower as well.

I could not find any information in the appraisal that mentioned where that income number was coming from. This report was some 50 pages long, and I read all of it! I asked the lender to ask the appraiser how he got those numbers, and he kept giving me weird answers that made no sense. Finally, three weeks later, I got the answer.

The appraiser had used one month of our financials to value the property. That month happened to be the month that the dance studio started, and we gave them a free month of rent. We were missing income from the dance studio, but even taking that away, the numbers he used were way too low. And then I saw what he did.

He deducted the interest from our loan from the income. You never count interest expense for a loan against the income of a property. This was a massive mistake. That was over $6,000 in income that should not have been deducted. With a 5.9% CAP rate, that equaled $1,220,000! Now I had my $4 million dollar valuation even with the dance studio not paying rent that month and not counting the land lease, which was another $2,500 a month. Based on his CAP rate this was a $5 million dollar building.

I told the banker all of this, and he passed it on the the appraiser. A couple weeks later, he came back with a new value of $3,950,000. This was close to the $4,000,000 that I was hoping for, but I still wondered how he came in so low based on the CAP rate.

This also shows that I should not have rented the place to myself for a cheap rate. Had I rented it at full-market rent, we would have had more income coming in, and the property would be worth much more money. True, I would have had to pay more rent, but half of that would have come back to me.

I looked through the revised appraisal, and he completely changed the way he calculated the income. Now, he was taking the full year's rent and deducting 3% for vacancies, 3% for leasing properties, and 15% for capital repairs. He was doing everything he could to come in low on this building. The property was in great shape, was fully leased, and the grocery store literally paid for any capital repairs on their side, which is most of the building.

I did not complain because I knew it was as good as it was going to get, but this appraisal had confirmed my thoughts on the value and let me know I was not crazy. It also showed I was being conservative with my cap rates and numbers which made me feel good about it all.

The banker congratulated me on getting the appraisal raised and said he would get to work on the loan. A week or so later, he called and said he wanted to meet with us to go over some options.

Every time a banker wants to meet in person, I feel they have bad news to deliver, and I was right.

After everything I had been through with the appraisal, the banker said they could only refinance what we bought it for plus any costs we put into the building. I made him explain why, and he emailed me all this crap about the building only increasing in value because of appreciation, how other banks are being super careful because of the housing crash, yada yada yada. I was pissed because I had told him from the very beginning he better not pull this again. I wrote him a not-so-nice email asking how adding $10,000 in income equals appreciation and have not heard from him since. I wonder now if the bank had pushed for a low appraisal because they knew they were only going to lend on costs.

If we were only able to refinance on costs alone, we would have a loan of maybe $1,650,000 instead of $3,000,000, and why even refinance at that point?

Luckily, I had somewhat expected this, and we had been talking to other banks. In fact, one bank had contacted us because they heard we wanted to refinance the building. I am not sure if they knew because I am a big mouth and talk about everything on social media or some other reason, but they knew.

I also had a number of other bank contacts I had used in the past and some from people I met through social media and my blogs. We got some offers, but most of them would not go up to the full 75%.

The problem was banks wanted to use a full year's financials, which meant we were not getting full credit for the new leases or the rent increases. Those banks were upfront about what they could offer from the beginning. We did find one that bank that said they could do the full $3,000,000 and another that would go up to $2,700,000. We are working to get the refinance done with the $3,000,000 loan now, and by the time this book is done, I am hoping to have an update and we have our money.

Continuing to add value

This has been an amazing property, and I think it will make us a lot of money. In fact, we have something lined up to greatly increase the revenue already.

One reason the property was so cheap to begin with was the grocery store paid a very low lease rate. They have been in the building for decades, and the previous owner cut them some very good deals.

Their lease is ending in 2022, and the owner of the store, who is in Texas, called me a few months ago to talk about extending the lease past 2022. He said they want to stay and were hoping to get something worked out.

I mentioned we would love for them to stay but that their rent was way below fair-market rents. I was a little scared because I did not want to lose this tenant. They occupied 52,000 of the 68,000 square feet. However, I knew that if they did leave, we could release the space and possibly break it up into smaller spaces with much higher rental rates. It would take some time, but if we were able to lease it out at full-market value, we could bring in $200,000 more a year, which would be $12,500 more in rent.

That would add $2,800,000 in value to the property, making it worth $7,000,000. That is based on a 7% CAP rate since I still want to be conservative with my numbers.

I did not tell the grocery store rep all of this, but he knew the property was leased well below market value. He told me he would run some numbers and see what they could do with the lease. I was ecstatic because he was going to make me an offer!

He called me a few days later and said they were willing to up their rent $5,000 a month starting in 2022, and they would up it $5,000 more in 2027, 2042, and 2037. I could not believe it because those were some serious increases.

I ran the numbers and figured out the store would still be well below market rent. That is how low their lease rate is. Even in 2032, when they would be paying $20,000 a month more than they are now, they would be right at market rent, but in 20 years, rents should be much higher due to inflation, so it would still be a good deal for the store, and they wouldn't have to move.

I negotiated a little and got them to increase their rents a little higher than their offer. When 2022 comes around, the value of the building will increase by more than $1,000,000 with their increased rental rates, and every five years after that it will increase by $1,000,000 again.

I love commercial real estate!

Don't forget, there are multiple videos of this property on YouTube. Just search for InvestFourMore and "rental number 21."

Update

Our refinance was approved, and we are close to closing on the loan with a 75% loan-to-value ratio at 3.99%.

27

Case Study #6: Vacant for How Long?

Rental property #22

It is going to be hard to follow that last property, but I will try with a property that has not done nearly as well.

Not every property is a home run, and this one is an example of that, although it still might turn out okay. This was a small restaurant I found on the MLS. It was listed for $110,000, which was super cheap, and I ended up making an offer without seeing it.

The property came up for sale on a Friday afternoon, and I was out of town or busy and had no time to see it. I knew the property because it was located on a very busy road right by the local college.

It was also located right by some major new development, including three brand-new apartment buildings going up with two blocks. They were high-end apartments and would completely change the area.

This property was a Mexican restaurant that had been in the area for decades.

I knew it well but had never eaten there. I knew where it was and knew it was cheap, and I decided to take my chances and make an offer without seeing it. I went a step further and made an offer with no inspection contingencies. Was I crazy? Maybe.

I made a full-price offer and got the property. Even with my fast offer, I beat out other offers according to the listing agent.

After buying the property, I learned the restaurant had closed due to health-code violations. They operated below the normal standards for restaurants for years because they were grandfathered in. But since the restaurant shut down, any new restaurant would have to upgrade everything to meet new codes.

The property was small—only 1,100 square feet—and some of that was a partially enclosed patio. The real kicker was the lot was about 1,200 square feet. I had no room to work with and had to stick with the existing building.

I had no plan for this property, but I knew it was in an awesome location. Every time I went to the restaurant, people were knocking on the door trying to buy burritos. I decided to try to fix it up a little and get it rented to a new restaurant.

I decided I had to talk to the city to see what was required for a new restaurant to operate. The health department met me there, and the first thing they asked was if I had seen any roaches yet. I had not, but I guess they had videos of roaches crawling all over, and that was the straw that broke the camel's back and shut them down.

The health department rep was very helpful, and he even thought I could put two restaurants in side by side to increase income. The problem was they could not give me exactly what needed to be done until they knew what kind of business would be moving in.

The property was very ugly, with peeling paint, outdated electrical, outdated plumbing, and a tiny grease trap that was basically a Tupperware bin. The bathroom was tiny and inaccessible to the public.

We had a lot of issues to work through. If a restaurant moved in that needed indoor seating, we would have to completely redo the bathroom and move it. If it was a restaurant that needed a big grease trap, major changes would have to be made, and the whole concrete floor would need to be ripped out. The kitchen would have to be reconfigured because there wasn't adequate room to move. Only a space heater kept the place warm, and there were broken windows.

I decided to fix the heat and market the property for lease as it was. We did not want to make many changes because it might all have to be redone once we knew what type of business would move in.

We advertised it and must have had 100 people contact us who wanted to start a restaurant over the last year. Yes, it has been a year, and it is still sitting there unoccupied. What is the problem?

We have talked to a number of people who want it. We tell them they need to talk to the city to figure out what will have to be done. They take their time or decide they don't want to move forward, and we start all over again. This has happened many times.

Recently, we have decided we might sell it and have talked to a few people with the same result. They go through this whole process of talking to the city and then decide they can't get the money together or don't want it.

It has gotten to the point where I might open my own restaurant! Not really—but I have thought of putting some type of business in the building.

The property has not cost me a ton of money, but it has just been sitting there while we pay taxes and insurance. To be honest, I am trying to sell for quite a bit more than I paid, so it won't be the worst investment if we do sell it.

The conundrum for me is that I know it is in an amazing location, and once these apartments are online many people will be within walking distance. It will be great for someone. I just don't know who yet.

While it is in a great location, it is not in the best location for a vacant building. Rocks have been thrown through windows twice, and a homeless guy broke in and was living there for a bit.

This has not been a home run, and it has not made me any money for more than a year. It still may be a good investment or might end up being something I decide to sell, take my medicine, and move on from.

28

Case Study #7: My First Mixed Use

Rental Property #23

I was hesitant to buy this property, but Nikki convinced me it would be a good deal. It was in the small town of Ault, near Greeley, where I do most of my investing. That town has about 1,000 people, which worried me a little. However, it's about 15 minutes from much larger towns.

The property was 2 stories and right on the main street. It was connected to other buildings and wasn't not very pretty. It had the old small-town two-story facade, but it was covered with weathered wood siding that looked a little like an old cabin.

The property had 4 units—3 residential and 1 commercial. Even though it was mostly residential, the one commercial unit makes it a a mixed-use property, and most banks considered it a commercial property for the sake of lending.

The property was listed for $220,000 on the MLS. I had thought about looking at it because it was so cheap. It is really hard to find a property for $220,000, let alone a four-unit mixed-use building. Cheap is not always better.

When I viewed the property, two residential units and the commercial unit were occupied. The commercial tenant paid $475 a month, and each residential unit paid $900 and $600 a month. The total rental income was $1,975. The vacant unit was a mess. A remodel was started but never finished, and it needed a lot of work.

It was a pretty good deal, even with one vacant unit. I could see the potential after viewing it. We could definitely increase the rents and finish out the last unit to add to the overall cash flow.

I talked to the listing agent, and she mentioned the seller was motivated. That is always a good sign, but being motivated can mean different things to different people. I decided to submit an offer that was quite a bit lower than asking price because of the property's condition.

I think I offered $180,000, which was pretty low. The agent called me and asked why I my offer was so low. I told her it was due to the seller being motivated. She was not put off and said she would talk to her seller to see what they could do.

She called back pretty quickly and told me the seller would go down to $193,500...but no lower. I said that would work for me, and we had a deal.

For this property, I used private money again. I financed the entire purchase price with a rate of 10%. Yes, I know that is a high rate, but private money can be very expensive. The trade off to the high rate is there is no appraisal or hoops to jump through, and I can literally text my lender, tell him what I want, and usually receive an OK.

My plan was to use private money for a year or so, stabilize the property, and then refinance it with a long-term bank loan. We closed on the property and got to work.

The first thing we did was fix up the vacant unit. It was an open space on the second floor and needed a lot of work. We took out the dropped ceiling, added a wall, redid the kitchen and bathroom, and made it a very nice one-bedroom unit. It was only 600 square feet, so it was a fairly easy rehab. I think we spent about $20,000.

We put it up for rent, and by "we," I mean Nikki. Nikki got a few responses right away and was able to rent it out for $800 a month.

There was also a larger three-bedroom unit on the main floor, or at least it was advertised as a three bedroom. Technically, it had only one bedroom as two of the bedrooms had no windows. It was rented for $900 a month, but those tenants moved out shortly after we bought it.

Ironically, the other occupied unit was a tiny 2 bedroom that was rented for $600 a month to a mother and her adult son. The mother had recently broken her hip, and she had to climb a lot of stairs. We freshened up the ground-floor vacant unit and rented it to them for $800 a month.

Why rent it for $800 instead of the original $900? We couldn't legally rent it out as a three-bedroom unit since it was technically a one-bedroom unit, and were able to refresh it for very little money. We also could rent it out right away without having to market it. The upstairs tenants could moved into the lower-level unit, which would help the mom out and give us time to refresh the upstairs unit.

We went to work on the upstairs unit and refreshed it as well. It was configured as a tiny two bedroom with dropped ceilings. We thought about completely remodeling the unit, but that would take twice as much money. We worked on the bath and kitchen and painted it. Nikki put that one up for rent, and it went for $1,000 a month!

All the units were now rented:

- Commercial hair salon: $475
- Lower level 1 bedroom: $800
- Upper 1 bedroom: $800
- Upper 2 bedroom: $1,000
- **Total $3,075**

By raising the rents and stabilizing the property, we had greatly increased the value. I think we spent about $50,000 on the repairs after painting the exterior and putting in other minor work.

If this was a straight commercial property with the tenants paying the expenses, it would be pretty easy to value, but the residential units make it a little tougher. We pay the water bill, the insurance, and the taxes, and there is usually more turnover with residential tenants and more maintenance costs, especially with lower-priced multi-unit tenants.

Property taxes were really cheap on this property—really cheap. I think we pay $800 a year, which is crazy. I think that is because the county thinks of it as residential property, and it is in a small town with low tax rates. Insurance is $2,000 dollars a year, and utilities are about $1,500 a year.

Without considering the other expenses that come with a property like this (maintenance and vacancies), we are looking at making about $32,000 a year in income. If you take into account vacancies and maintenance, we are closer to $25,000. That is still a fantastic number for a property I bought for $193,500!

If we use CAP rates the property would be worth $357,000 based on a 7% CAP rate. I think that CAP rate is very accurate based on the small town and the property. To be conservative, we might need to use an 8% CAP rate, which would make it worth $312,500.

My plan was to refinance the property after we got it leased. I started talking to one of the banks that had helped me out before, but they had some reservations. Some of my flips had not gone so well at the time, and I was buying multiple properties. They were worried that my debt-to-income ratio was getting too high and did not want to do the refinance.

While you often hear that multifamily or commercial real estate lending is all based on the property, and the owner can have bad credit and no income, that is not entirely true. The lenders don't want to lend to credit risks.

I think I am just fine to lend to, but I was starting to hit certain thresholds with the banks because of all the properties I own and all the loans. I was a little annoyed because it was so easy to get some of my loans in the past. I am not even sure if this bank had asked for my tax returns for my first loan. Maybe that was the problem, and the lender got in trouble because he did not have all the right docs.

I did some searching and found a national lender who said they would do the deal. They claim they really do not care about debt-to-income ratios. My credit is over 800, and I have never missed a payment in my life, so I thought I was a pretty good candidate. They were worried about one unit being commercial because they almost always only loan on residential, but since the commercial unit was so small, they said they would do the deal.

That is one drawback to commercial real estate: getting loans can be tougher because fewer lender will loan on straight commercial properties. Not only would this lender be willing to do the loan, but they also offered 30-year fixed products. That means I could hold the loan for 30 years without the rate ever going up or them calling the loan due. The catch was the rate was slightly higher at 5.5% instead of less than 5%. Since the amortization is 30 years instead of 20 or 25, my payment would be about the same.

I was hoping the property would appraise for $350,000, but I would be fine with $325,000 or even $300,000. If it appraised for $350,000, I could get a loan for $262,500, and if it appraised for $300,000, I could get a loan for $225,000. My payment would either be $1,490 with the higher loan amount or $1,277 with the lower. That payment would be lower than my interest-only loan payment of $1,612, and a portion of the new payment would be going towards the loan as well.

If I got this deal refinanced, I would be cash flowing $600 to 800 dollars a month and have less than a $20,000 invested in the property. I would also have about $100,000 in equity. This was looking like a great deal.

Then it happened. As we were looking at options for the appraisal, one of the tenants had some major issues. There were some domestic problems, and the tenants moved out, leaving a few holes in the walls. This was the unit that we just rented out for $1,000 a month.

I did not want to get an appraisal with one vacant unit. I put everything on hold. We made some minor repairs, and we put it up for rent again. Nikki was working on getting it rented out when we realized she was spending too much time on property management. She was still managing all of my flips as well.

We turned the management over to a property manager since it contained mostly residential units, and that freed up more of our time. Hopefully it's rented soon, and we can complete the refinance at that time.

Maybe by the time this book is published, I can update you with some good news.

Update

Shortly after writing this, another tenant moved out. We had two vacant units, but the property manager was able to get both units rented out fairly quickly and for more than we were getting before.

29

Case Study #8: History in the Making

Rental Property #24

I love this property, and it has a ton of value-add potential. I bought this one in late 2019, and we are still working on stabilizing it. We did a lot of interesting things on this deal, including completing a 1031 exchange on a very tight schedule.

This was another property from the MLS. It was listed months before I even looked at it. I had seen it come up for sale, and it seemed like a good deal at $625,000 for 10,000 square feet. That was great, but it was a very old building built in 1927. It was occupied by a fence company.

When this first came up for sale, I asked my partner from rental number 21 if he was interested in this one. I had been buying a lot of properties, and I did not have a ton of cash to throw at this property. I would need at least $150,000 for the down payment and more for closing costs.

My partner was not very interested in the property, and I had many other things going on, so I let it go for the time being. A few months later, it popped back up on the MLS because it had gone under contract but the deal fell apart.

I was much more interested in the property the second time around. I had been looking at my residential properties and noticed how much equity I had in them, but they were not making much money compared to all that equity.

I bought my first residential property for $96,900 in 2010, and it was currently worth $275,000. It rented for $1,050 when I first bought it, and when it was worth $275,000, it was renting for $1,500 a month. I had refinanced that property at one point, but I had about $150,000 in equity. I was making maybe $600 a month after all expenses, which is a 4.8% return on equity.

I began to think that I could use the equity in my residential rentals to buy properties that would generate much more money. The tenants were leaving this property soon. We could refresh it and sell it, and I could 1031 exchange it into a new property. I could use the 1031 exchange money as the down payment and have the cash to do this deal on my own. It would be the most expensive property I had ever purchased without a partner.

I decided to take a look art the property and get all the details. There was probably a reason it was so cheap and was still for sale.

I talked to the listing agent, and there was a reason it was so cheap. The fence company was renting the entire space for $2,800 a month. That was about 1/3 of what market rent should be for that space. The agent also said the last deal fell through because the buyer could not get financing for the property because the rent rate was so low.

That was a problem for me because I was planning to get a bank loan to buy this property. Luckily, I had some other options. I talked to my partner and asked if he wanted to do a private loan on this one for $450,000 or so. He said he would love to, and then when he saw how good of a deal it was, he tried to become a partner on the property, but it was too late for that.

I had my financing lined up, and I had a way to get the money for the down payment. Technically, I could get the money together for the down payment, but I like to keep quite a bit of cash available. Property flipping takes takes a lot of money, and it is easy to run out if you are not careful!

I viewed the property, and it was a fantastic building. Yes, it was old, but it had an incredible brick exterior and was on the busiest corner in town and had two extra lots for parking and storage.

My biggest problem was the rent the fence company was paying. There was no way $2,800 a month would pay the loan and expenses on this property. It could also take some time to rent it out again if the fence company left. The listing agent told me the seller knew the tenant and wanted to make sure I was not going to kick him out if I bought the property. I could see why it had not sold yet.

The tenant was an incredibly nice guy and super helpful. He told me all about the building and was very open about his lease and knew it was was too cheap. I decided to talk to him about upping what he paid to see if he was open to it.

He was very open to it, and he knew if he had to move, it would a giant pain since the entire building was full of his supplies. He also could not find any properties that were available to rent at a reasonable rate.

Since he was open to increasing the rent, I made an offer. I think I offered $575,000, and they countered at $602,000. I accepted, and we were under contract.

I had a lot of work to do. I was going to do an inspection to make sure there were not any major problems, I had to get my rental property ready to sell, and I had to negotiate a new lease with the fence company.

The first thing I did was bring in remodelers on my rental. I had 90 days to close on this property and asked the seller to take part in a 1031 exchange, but the seller was not keen on that idea. They did not want any delays. Even though they did not want to do a 1031 exchange, I was going to try to get one done anyway. I could also do a reverse 1031 exchange if I had to, but this property first, and sell my rental later. The problem with the reverse exchange is that it is much more expensive, and I have to come up with the down payment first and then get reimbursed from the sale of the exchanged property.

We fixed up my rental and put it on the market right away. We listed it for $289,900, which I thought was a fair price, but we got no action the first ten days. We lowered the price to $284,000 and still had no action for two weeks. We lowered the price again to $274,000. At that point, we received two offers right away. We asked for highest and best. One offer was $275,000 and they wanted to close right away (within 3 weeks), which was awesome.

I did not do a full inspection because I was only worried about a few things. The seller had already completed a phase 1 and phase 2 environmental report, which was nice, but again, I am not that concerned with those reports. The reports showed there had been an underground tank at one time because it used to be a gas station. The tank had been removed and cleaned up, so I was good there.

I sent my roofer and HVAC guy to look at the property, and that was it. The nice thing about using them is they don't charge me. The HVAC looked decent. The roof was newer, but it had not been done correctly, and it would eventually need some work. I talked with the tenant, and he said they had never had any leaks, so it did not seem to be an urgent issue.

I still knew I would have to do some work on the roof. I asked the seller to take $15,000 off the price, and he agreed to take $10,000 off. I was cool with that.

Then I had to deal with the lease and the tenant. In fact, the seller wanted me to work out a new before he would sell the property to me. I calculated what the market rent would be if I were to rent it to a new tenant. I reduced that amount to give the tenant some incentive to stay, which would make it easier on both of us.

I was hoping he would be cool with the new numbers, even though they were much higher than what he was paying. Ultimately, he decided the new rent was too high and would not work. He asked how much time he would have to find a new place. I was super disappointed.

I was not giving up yet because the tenant had told me he would be willing to reduce the space he used. He didn't need much of the stuff that was lying around. I offered to rent him half the building at a slightly higher rate than I had offered him for the entire building. He agreed.

The financing, 1031 exchange, new lease, and inspection were out of the way. But, the deal was not done because the rental I was selling was set to close two weeks before I bought the new property.

When that date neared, the agent for the buyers of my rental said they needed more time. Ugh. They said the buyers were solid and could close fast, which is why we took—that, and it was higher than the other one—but anyway they still said they could close right away.

They wanted to delay closing to the day before I bought the other property. This was not the end of the world, but it could cause some problems. I asked the seller to extend the timeline by week, and they would not do it. They said they needed to close right away, which is why they didn't want to do a 1031 exchange in the first place.

So, I had to get creative. I told the seller I would give them $2,500 if they extended by a week. They agreed, and the buyers closed on the same day we were supposed to buy the new property. It was a good thing I extended because there was no way we could send the proceeds from the 1031 exchange to the 1031 exchange company and then have the 1031 exchange company send the money to the title company for closing. I paid $2,500 for one day, but it made the deal work, and everyone was happy.

After we closed, the tenant and I signed a three-year lease for half of the building. He was happy, and I could now try to rent out the other side. With the new lease from the fence company, I was making enough money to break even on the property every month, and another new lease would all go to profit.

We cleaned up the other side and advertised it. I have not had too many problems leasing out properties in the past, but you never know with commercial real estate. We closed in September, and it has yet to be rented. It is large, with 4,700 square feet, and we have been willing to split it into 2 smaller spaces, but we haven't had any luck.

A few have expressed interest, but they have been in no hurry to get a deal done. I am hoping we can get this space leased out soon, but that is something to consider with commercial spaces and is why I was worried about this property from the beginning. That is also why I wanted the fence company to stay. At least the entire building wasn't vacant.

If we do get the other side leased for close to what we want, we will be making enough to make this a million-dollar-plus property. Then, I plan to refinance, pay off the private lender, and take a lot of cash back out. If we get a 75% loan-to-value mortgage, I would have a $750,000 loan, and I would get back more than $300,000 after paying the private lender.

This is a great property, but making value-add deals perform takes some work.

30

Case Study #9: Don't Ignore the Small Deals

Rental property number 25

I also bought this property from the MLS. It still boggles my mind how many good deals I have gotten from the MLS on commercial rentals when so many people tell you getting a good deal there is impossible.

This property had been listed for almost a year when I finally decided to make an offer. When it first when up for sale, it was listed at $175,000. It had 1,680 square feet and was on a very busy one-lane street in my hometown. The property was most recently used as a pawn shop.

I was interested when it first came on the market. However, the price was not quite good enough for me since I had bought similar-sized properties closer to $100,000. After 6 months, the price on this dropped to $159,900.

I still was not quite on board, but it never sold. A few months later, I kept a closer eye on it and finally decided to take a look at it. The first time I tried to view it, the agent did not call me back for quite some time. He was a residential agent and did not do too many deals. He finally called and told us we could see it. He said the lock box was next to the front door, but we didn't find it.

We tried a few weeks later and found the lock box. The place was mostly empty, with only a few remnants of the pawn shop. It wasn't in horrible shape, but it needed some work. The roof also leaked.

I knew this could be a good rental, but it was in a worse area than most of my other properties. I was not sure how hard it would be to rent out since there was another vacant property for sale right next to it. That property was 2,500 square feet and listed for $230,000.

I ran my numbers and decided to make an offer of $110,000. I usually do not offer that much lower than the listing price, but the property had been for sale for a very long time, and I thought that might motivate the sellers.

They sent me a counter for $130,000, which I thought was decent. I accepted.

I used private financing for this property as well. You may think I would be running out of people to borrow money from, but my lenders have some deep pockets. This business requires good connections.

We rehabbed it, and most of the money went to the roof. I think we spent $15,000 on the roof because they had to rebuild part if it so that it would drain properly. We also tore out some old counters, replaced the ceiling tiles, and painted the walls. We tore out the ugly carpet but did not put any flooring in yet.

My reasoning for not putting in flooring yet was a new tenant may want to change the floor plan. If they change the floor plan and we put new flooring in, we may have to rip it all out again. We usually use commercial-grade laminate flooring in our commercial properties.

Once the repairs were complete, we put it up for rent. It is not rented yet, but it has only been on the market a few weeks. By the time you read this, I hope to have good news on at least one of these properties.

Update

This was up for rent for about a month when we received an offer. This all happened at the start of the COVID-19 lockdown. We settled on $1,650 a month, and I signed the leases, but the tenants backed out at the last minute because many in their business lost their jobs.

31

Case Study #10: "The Compound"

Rental Property Number 26

This my scariest commercial rental property, and many people wonder why I bought it. It was listed on Loopnet off and on for quite a while before I decided to make an offer.

This property had four buildings, 4 very old houses and an old commercial store. None of the properties were in great shape, but they were all occupied.

The interesting thing about this property is it is right on a very busy four-lane highway. That would be a bad location for houses, but it has development potential. It has over an acre of land, and it is zoned as light commercial. It is located in the city of Evans, and they plan to make this corridor a trendy commercial hub.

I give the city credit for being positive and having vision, but right now, most of the corridor is industrial. The listing agent was very upfront about the zoning and even said he was not sure I could keep the houses since the city really wants them demolished.

Before I made an offer, I called the city. They said they would not make us demolish the houses, but eventually, they would love to see it be redeveloped. To be clear, I do not want to be the one who redevelops this property.

I am buying it because it can be a cash-flow monster and is a fantastic deal. Housing is expensive in Colorado, and it is hard to find a property for less than $200,000 in the area.

The houses are small. Two have two bedrooms and one has one bedroom. They are old, and the property was strewn with trash, vehicles, and junk when I saw it. The commercial property was brick and occupied by a car-repair business. The agent again was upfront and said he did not think that was a legal use and the city might kick them out.

All of this was listed for $430,000. The commercial building alone, if rented right, was worth close to that price. The houses were like a bonus, or they may detract from the value depending on how you look at it. Nikki was one of the people who didn't think this purchase was a good idea I guess we will find out who is right!

I made an offer of $390,000, and they countered at $410,000, which I accepted. I wanted to complete a 1031 exchange. I had a vacant rental in an area experiencing much turnover. The rent was $1,500 a month, and I had $180,000 in equity.

We had to make some repairs before we sold it. When you sell residential properties, it helps to make them turn key ready. It also helps if they are vacant because most buyers want to live in the house. When you rent out a property, it does not have to be quite as nice as when you sell it. When we sell our rentals, we often have to fix them up.

I had 110 days to get the closing done on this property, and this time, the seller was fine with a 1031 exchange. This property went under contract right away.

We asked $274,900 and received multiple offers, the best being $275,000.

We had no problems with lenders this time around, but the appraiser came in with a value of $270,000. This happens frequently. I usually challenge the appraisal if it comes in low, but we were in a time crunch, so I accepted the lower $270,000 price.

I had about $175,000 in proceeds I could use towards the new property, and I got a private loan for $230,000. If these numbers don't seem to add up, remember I pay earnest money when I make the offer, and that earnest money is applied to the purchase.

I now owned another wonderful property. The houses were bringing in $600, $650, and $700 in monthly rent, and the commercial tenant was paying $1,600 a month. I was bringing in over $3,500 a month on this property from the start, which is not bad considering $410,000 price.

Of course, I did not know when I bought it that basically none of the residential tenants were paying rent. When we told them where to send the checks, they said they never paid rent before. Some of them did not even know how much the rent was.

It turns out the seller and most of the people living there were related or knew each other in one way or another. Getting this property sorted out has been challenging to say the least. We've successfully collected rent from one residential tenant, and the shop is current. The other two have paid a little, but it's been nothing close to what they owe.

The kicker is their rent is extremely low. The lowest rent in the area is about $500 a month, and the average is $1,200. If these tenants try to find a new place, they are going to be in trouble. We are trying to work with them since I am sure the seller did not tell them what was going on.

Finding new tenants will not be the end of the world since they are paying such low rent. It may be tough to rent out these houses, but we could spend some money on them and get at least $1,000 each, if not more, and that accounts for the houses being right next to the highway.

If we were to rent them out for that, we would have $4,600 coming in monthly, making this deal look better and better. The commercial space is underpriced too, but I am not looking to find a new tenant right away for that property.

The plan with this property is to keep it as a rental as it is for a while and eventually, if development takes off, possibly sell it for a huge profit. It is in an opportunity zone and is a great location for commercial.

Update

We started evictions, all with a cash-for-keys agreement. We were going to pay them $500 to leave. When that was happening, COVID-19 hit, and all evictions were put on hold and the other tenants decided not to leave. We shall see how this progresses!

IV

My Future Plans

32

My Plan to Buy One Million Square Feet of Rentals

In 2013, I set a goal to buy 100 rental properties. I created this plan because I wanted a huge goal that would push and motivate me. I have not come close to reaching that goal, mostly because I stopped buying houses when the market increased so much in Colorado. In 2017, I started buying commercial real estate. While I have only bought 26 rentals so far, one of those has 68,000 square feet, and I think that counts for more than a property or two.

When I wrote my plan, it came from my barely legible notebooks where I calculated how much cash flow and net worth I would have each year from my properties. Those writings while cumbersome, were incredibly motivating and implanted that goal in my head. I have not written anything that detailed in many years, and I thought it would be fun to try setting a new goal. Due to my success with commercial real estate, I have decided I want to buy 1,000,000 square feet in rental properties by 2029.

Why set a ten-year goal?

I hate to admit this or even think about it, but I'll turn 50 in 2029. Turning 40 was crazy enough, but I know I can't do anything about that. If I am going to be that old, I might as well set a pretty awesome goal to go along with it.

I like to set short- and long-term goals. The long-term goals often set the path for the short-term goals and give me a clear idea of what I am shooting for. A ten-year plan gives me an idea of what I need to do each year. My yearly goals give me an idea of what I need to do each month. And, my monthly goals give me an idea of what I need to do each week.

I love looking at the big picture because if I tell myself what I want my life to look like, I have a much better shot of living how I want. If you have no idea what you are doing in life, it is very hard to get what you want. I can guarantee you will achieve your ideas, but that may not be what you want from life. A long-term plan gives you a road map for your life.

If your life does not go exactly as planned, it's OK. There will be roadblocks and detours, but you are so much better off starting with a plan than randomly doing things and hoping things work out. My plan to buy 100 houses has not worked out exactly as I thought it would, but it still helped me tremendously, and I know I have done much more because of that plan than I would have without it.

How many rentals and how much square footage do I have now?

I just bought my 26th rental property, which is mixed-use and has a commercial building and three houses. They add up to 2,600 square feet. I had about 118,000 square feet before this purchase, but I also used a 1031 exchange to buy this property, and in the process, I sold a 1,600-square-foot property. I gained 5,100 square feet and lost 1,600 for a net of 3,500. I now have 121,500 square feet.

I know you may be thinking owning 1,000,0000 square feet will take a long time at this pace. However, I bought three other buildings this year that were 10,500, 1,600, and 2,500 square feet. I ended up buying 19,700 square feet and selling about 3,000 since I 1031 exchanged another rental as well. Last year, I bought two rentals totaling 69,000 square feet.

It will take 878,500 more square feet to reach my goal. That seems crazy to me now, but many of the things I have accomplished would seem crazy to me ten years ago.

How do you work a goal backward?

How can you possibly work towards something like my goal? You have to work it backwards. I have 9 years to complete this goal, so I would need:

- 97,600 square feet each of the next 9 years
- 24,400 square feet each quarter
- 8,100 square feet each month

That is still a lot of square footage to buy each month and year. However, I do not have to buy the same amount each year. I assume things will continue to get better, and I will learn more each year. I can start out buying less square footage and increase what I buy every year.

I could buy 50,000 square feet in 2020 and then up that amount each year:

- 2020: 50k square feet
- 2021: 70k square feet
- 2022: 90k square feet
- 2023: 110k square feet
- 2024: 130k square feet
- 2025: 150k square feet
- 2026: 170k square feet

- 2027: 190k square feet
- 2028: 210k square feet
- 2029: Goal reached

In the end, I'll have bought 1,170,000 square feet, and I only needed 878,500. I can reduce those numbers by almost 300k and still reach my goal. Now, things are looking much more attainable, and I even stopped buying before 2029!

Why make the goal 1,000,000 square feet?

I have mentioned this goal on the InvestFourMore Instagram page a few times, and many people comment that it seems like a strange goal. Why one million square feet? What does that even mean? I agree it is a little strange since I could buy 1,000,000 square feet of junk somewhere that generates no money. However, I love this goal for a few reasons:

- It is exciting to think about 1 million square feet. I love goals that excite me because they stick in my mind and I constantly think about them.
- This goal is easy to measure. I will know for sure whether I hit this goal or not and how I am doing along the way.
- The goal is great for marketing. Yes, I sell books and coaching and love to promote this website. This goal gets people talking and is a real attention grabber.
- I have always been very good about only buying home-run deals. I very rarely buy a rental that won't generate money and be a good investment. I know that I won't buy a bunch of junk to hit this goal.
- I will have to work very hard to reach this goal because it is so big and challenging. This goal should help my business tremendously.

I love big, exciting goals. The best goal I ever set was to buy a Lamborghini Diablo back in 2014. That was so motivating and helped my business in so many ways. It made me think outside of the box and focus on constant improvement.

How much square footage will I buy each year?

The first thing I want to mention is this is a guideline, not a set schedule. Some years, I may buy much more than my plan, and others, I may buy much less. In the end, I am hoping that the years play out like this:

2020

I plan to buy 50,000 square feet of rentals, and I already have 25,000 square feet under contract. I don't want to go too crazy my first year as I only bought about 20,000 square feet in 2019, so this will be challenging. In 2018, I bought way more than 50,000 square feet, but again this is about the big picture, not being exact each year.

2021

I plan to buy 60,000 square feet. Again, this should be challenging, but I think it is doable. I could buy one big property and hit this goal, or I could buy 5 smaller properties and hit it. You may be asking how can I afford to keep buying so many properties. I flip 20 to 30 houses a year and make decent money from that business. I can also refinance these properties after adding value to pull cash out to buy more.

2022

I plan to buy 70,000 square feet. Do you see a trend yet? It is a simple plan, but it will still be difficult to keep buying big properties like this every year. I also cannot foresee any big changes in the economy or my own business. If the economy does change, it may create more buying opportunities as well, although it might make it harder to finance properties.

2023

I will buy 80,000 square feet. This will put me at 260,000 square feet in new purchases and 380,000 total. Right now, I am making about $125 a month per 1,000 square feet from rentals I own (with some inefficiencies like vacant units). If I am able to continue that trend, I will be making $47,500 a month from my rentals. That will be another way I can earn money to buy more rentals.

2024

I will buy 100,000 square feet, bringing my total to 480,000. I am almost halfway to my goal with 4 to 5 years left. This shows me that I can actually buy less than this plan outlines and have a great shot at hitting this goal. I could make up for a slow start by purchasing more properties in the later years.

2025

I will buy 110,000 square feet, bringing the total to 590,000. I will continue to add value and refinance to pull cash out. By this point, who knows if I even need to flip houses anymore, although I have to admit I love flipping and may never stop.

2026

I will buy 120,000 square feet, bringing my total to 710,000. When I bought my 68,000-square-foot strip mall, I used a partner. That is the only time I have used a partner to buy a rental. I may be using a partner to buy some of these bigger properties, but I would love to continue to buy properties on my own if I can.

2027

I will add 130,000 square feet. This would be about double what I have bought before. I am hoping, by this time, I will have tons of cash lying around just waiting for the right properties. I should be in a position to take on some bigger projects that are a little riskier but have huge value add potential.

2028

I will buy 140,000 square feet, which will make my total 980,000. I will be making $122,500 a month based on the dollar-per-square-foot I am making now. Although, by this time, inflation will have caused rents to increase, and I will most likely be making much more than that.

2029

I only need to buy 20,000 more square feet to hit my goal. I should have a lot of money coming in from these properties and be set for quite a while. I could focus on paying off debt if I wanted or just continue to buy more properties since I seem to be addicted to the process.

What will my rental-property portfolio look like?

I have no idea exactly what kind of properties I will have or where they will be or how much equity I'll have, but it is always fun to guess. My properties are worth close to $100 a square foot right now, maybe slightly less. I have about a 60% debt-to-value ratio (for every $1,000,000 in rentals, I owe about $600,000 to banks).

- If I own one million square feet, my properties would be worth around 100 million dollars or more due to inflation.
- I will have about $60,000,000 in debt, although I could see this being less since we will be paying off loans over time, and I assume I will not

have to refinance every property to pull cash out as time goes on and we build cash up.

- I will be making well more than $100,000 a month and most likely close to $150,000 a month.
- This is all without syndicating or bringing in tons of equity partners.

Seeing this in writing is pretty cool, and I did not have all of these numbers before writing this section.

Conclusion

Big goals are amazing, and they have helped me out all through my career. I had been feeling a little unmotivated and stuck in a rut lately, and setting this goal really helped me focus on the big picture and create something to shoot for. Will I hit this goal? Maybe. Maybe not. But, trying it will be fun, and I know having a specific goal like this will help me do more than if I was just floating along hoping for the best.

33

New Deals and Missed Deals

I continue to buy more properties and look for new deals. Some of them didn't work out for a number of reasons. I will go over a few of those and why they did not work out.

Deal under contract

I have a new deal under contract that is very exciting and new to me. I am venturing outside my market to buy a smoking deal, or at least I hope it is.

This new property is 90 miles east in Sterling, where properties are much cheaper. I found the property thanks to my team, Nikki, and my nephew Alex, who works with me. They both have had their eye on Sterling for various reasons. While looking at some other deals, I saw a 25,000-square-foot warehouse for sale for $260,000.

I ended up getting it under contract for $240,000 and negotiating that down to $230,000. I close on that soon, probably by the time this book is published. I do not know what I am going to do with this property yet, but I plan to rent it out in some way. Maybe I'll convert it to storage units, one big company, or RV storage.

I did buy this in the middle of the COVID-19 crisis for $230,000. The video of it is on the InvestFourMore YouTube channel.

Deals that fell through

A deal I had under contract with my partner recently fell apart. It was a large commercial building in Greeley, and the sellers wanted $1,999,000. It was listed at 20,000 square feet and had 4.5 acres zoned for outside storage.

The downside to this property was it needed work and was vacant. It was built in the 1960s and was a cool-looking property with a modified A-frame construction. I think it could have been split into smaller units and rented out pretty quickly.

My partner and I talked about the property for a while before we decided to make an offer. He was worried about getting it rented out and the costs to fix it up. I was concerned about that as well but thought it could be a three-million-dollar property after all was said and done.

We offered them $1,500,000 because it was vacant and needed work. I knew this was a low offer, and I was prepared for them to turn it down or counter much higher. The listing agent called me a few days later and talked to me for a while. He said the seller was willing to come down to $1,687,000, and I replied that should work.

He sent us a new offer with the new price but said the seller could not sign it yet since he was out of town. We signed the contract and sent it back to the listing agent. A few days passed and nothing came back from the seller. Then, the listing agent called me with interesting news—the seller decided he wanted to raise the price to $1,800,000.

What? I was a little angry since the agent had verbally stated the price and even sent a new offer. I didn't know if the seller was playing games or the agent never got confirmation on the price.

I decided to move forward with the higher price knowing I still had my inspection period to check the property out. During the inspection period, we brought a few people in to look at the major systems. While we were looking at the property, I was measuring how big smaller units would be, and my intuition kept telling me something was wrong.

I took all the measurements and added the square footage up. I did not come close to getting 20,000, I got 17,000. I bought one of those measuring sticks with wheels. I came up with 17,000 again.

I checked public records, which stated 20,000 square feet as well. I visited the property and saw the problem. It had 10-foot overhangs on two sides. The county and the listing counted those overhangs as interior square footage when it was exterior space.

Not only did that greatly affect the value, but the seller had been paying taxes on the wrong square footage for decades. Based on the wrong square footage and the condition of the property, we asked for a price drop to $1,500,000.

The seller said they would come down to $1,675,000, but that was not good enough for us, and the deal died. Looking back, I am glad we did not buy that place since it needed a lot of work, and renting it out would have taken a lot of time. It would have been really tough to get financing, and we would have had a ton of money tied up in it for years.

Another deal that fell through was a massive property. After I cancelled this deal, my sister told me she was glad I did not buy it because she thought it would sink me. It was an old Hewlett Packard building that had 250,000 square feet and had been vacant for at least 15 years.

I got the property under contract for around $2.5 million and started investigating what it would take to buy the property and split it up into smaller spaces. I even had two contractors give me bids to fix it up. Those bids came in at close to $6 million just to do the main floor excluding the upstairs.

Aside from those bids, the seller had sold another part of the property to a school and leased land that basically cut off the access to the big building. I knew this deal would not work for me.Plus, I would have to raise a lot of money!

I talked to the city about tax incentives and uses. I talked to lenders. I even had architectural drawings made up. I did a lot of work. Some might think it was wasted time, but I learned a ton, and that building helped jump start my commercial investing.

Just because a deal does not work out does not mean it was a waste of time. Failed deals can help you along your journey.

34

Finishing Thoughts on Commercial Real Estate

I am a fairly new commercial real estate investor in the grand scheme of things. I have been through a really rough housing market, but only on the residential side. I have seen what happened to many commercial properties during the recession, but I did not own any of them at the time.

I would love to tell you that commercial real estate is always great and there will never be any problems. However, it can be affected by downturns more than residential can. People will always need a place to live, but they will not always need a space to operate a business. Some businesses may close during a downturn.

I would be lying if I said that commercial was not riskier than residential. It can be harder to lease, have more liability, and be hit harder when the economy takes hit. However, the upsides can be amazing, and those upsides outweigh the risks for me. You will have to decide if those upsides outweigh the risk for you.

Also, your market will dictate what the best business is for you. In some areas, many vacant commercial properties cannot be given away yet have a massive shortage of residential properties. Or, you could invest in an area with a massive shortage of commercial properties.

It is also important to remember that commercial properties can have a wide range of uses, and you can often change the use if you lose a big tenant. You can convert to smaller units or turn big buildings into storage units. I personally do not like to depend on one tenant to generate all of my money on a property.

As you can see from my case studies, I also make sure I get a great deal with plenty of upside potential on anything I buy. I do not pay market prices for stabilized properties since I don't see that as wealth creation but rather as wealth preservation.

I can see why large commercial investors often prefer stabilized properties because they offer less risk and require less work than value-add properties require.

One of the best things about value-add commercial real estate is there is not nearly as much competition for it as for residential real estate. Many investors are looking to flip homes or are looking for multifamily residential properties in just about every market. Far fewer investors are willing to take on commercial real estate, and you don't have to do massive deals to get good prices.

If you are just starting out in the investing world, I don't suggest jumping into commercial real estate unless you have some experienced people on your team to help you and plenty of cash to resolve issues and unknowns that will come up.

Market changes from a complete unknown

After writing this book, we have run into something that the world has never seen in our lifetime—a virus that has completely shut things down. As I write this, in April of 2020, things seem to be getting better, but we still have a long way to go before we are through with the virus and the economic impacts.

My properties have done fairly well so far, but it helps that my biggest tenant is a grocery store. I have a restaurant that has also done well, relatively speaking, thanks to their takeout business. The coffee shop has done well, but the dance studio is shut down for now. I think about them all the time and the struggles they must be going through.

Most of my commercial renters have been doing well, but in Colorado, many businesses are considered essential and can keep working. I think this economic shutdown will have a huge impact on commercial real estate, but it is too early to know what kind of impact. More people could be working from home. There may be fewer restaurants. Many business could close for good.

While people losing their businesses and livelihood is horrible, there will also be great opportunity. There will also be plenty of government aid for businesses that struggle. I just hope most of that aid makes it to the right people!

If you own commercial real estate, you must be more flexible now than ever. You must be willing to accommodate different types of tenants and make your properties stand out from the others. This time also shows how important it is to have cash reserves, no matter what business you are in!

www.ingramcontent.com/pod-product-compliance
Lightning Source LLC
Chambersburg PA
CBHW030612220526
45463CB00004B/1265